Narrating the Past

Narrating the Past:
(Re)Constructing Memory, (Re)Negotiating History

Edited by

Nandita Batra and Vartan P. Messier

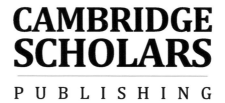

CAMBRIDGE SCHOLARS

PUBLISHING

Narrating the Past: (Re)Constructing Memory, (Re)Negotiating History,
Edited by Nandita Batra and Vartan P. Messier

This book first published 2007. The present binding first published 2009.

Cambridge Scholars Publishing

12 Back Chapman Street, Newcastle upon Tyne, NE6 2XX, UK

British Library Cataloguing in Publication Data
A catalogue record for this book is available from the British Library

ISBN (10): 1-4438-0170-4, ISBN (13): 978-1-4438-0170-6

TABLE OF CONTENTS

Part III: Narrating Women

PREFACE

Established over forty years ago, the Caribbean Chapter of the College English Association is a branch of the national College English Association in the United States, an organization with several regional chapters all across North America. Its mission is to promote the teaching of college-level English, each regional chapter operating independently. Throughout the years, conferences hosted by the Caribbean Chapter (which is known as the CEA-CC) have tended to focus on literary and cultural themes in addition to pedagogical ones. The CEA-CC has attracted participants from a wide geographical radius, a radius that has been amplified since the advent of the Internet. Although topics addressed at CEA-CC conferences do not solely focus on Caribbean issues, they nevertheless provide an optimum forum for both Caribbean and international scholars to discuss such issues from a variety of approaches. This has allowed us to develop and promote a dynamic forum where students and scholars in the Caribbean can be stimulated by international scholars to present, share and discuss their academic interests and research projects, and vice-versa. Consequently, we felt it would be a shame not to have some permanent record of these symposia, and it was with this goal in mind that we began publishing the proceedings of our conferences. Following the success of *Transgression and Taboo: Critical Essays*, the first CEA-CC publication, this volume represents our second publication as an association. "Narrating the Past: (Re)Constructing Memory, (Re)Negotiating History" was the topic of the CEA-CC Fall 2005 conference,[1] which included presentations by scholars from the Caribbean, the U.S., Europe, and the Middle East.

---

[1] We thank those who helped in organizing, especially José Jiménez Justiniano, Thea Leticia Mateu and Stéphane Pillet.

Narration, Memory, History: An Introduction

Vartan P. Messier and Nandita Batra

> Narrative is present in every age, in every place, in every society; it begins with the very history of mankind and there nowhere is nor has been people without narrative.
>
> Roland Barthes, "Introduction to the Structural Analysis of Narratives"

Narrative, as Barthes reminds us, constitutes an integral part of human existence, being omnipresent in our ordering of the world and the ways in which we transmit both knowledge and experience. For instance, Paul Ricoeur has argued that it is only through narrative that the abstract concept of time becomes human time and that hence, if we are able to confer meaning and credibility on events, it is by placing them in the time/space continuum that narrative structure provides. Likewise, recognizing the etymological link between 'narrating' and 'knowing' (while the former comes from the Latin *narrare*, to tell, both can be traced back to the Indo-European root *gna*), Hayden White has argued that narrative might be a "solution to a problem of general human concern, namely, the problem of how to translate *knowing* into *telling*" ("Value" 5). One could say then, that most attempts to communicate knowledge take the form of a narrative: of shaping events, be they laws of physics, mathematical formulations, incidental anecdotes, or everyday occurrences, into a *sequence of events*, or in broader terms, into a *story*.

The pull towards shaping events—or rather, as Michel Foucault would put it in poststructuralist terms, the "statements of events"—into comprehensible and/or logical form, is particularly pervasive when attempting to communicate knowledge of the past, especially as the past serves as a tool for understanding the present and possibly envisioning the future: from the self-shaping narrative of personal identity to the collective narratives that define a culture or nation.[1] In fact, the intersection of various historical narratives has played a crucial role in the transnational exchanges brought forth by globalization and the push to deconstruct and redefine national boundaries and identities. Personal, national, and hybrid identities have all been forged through the collection, construction, and dissemination of narratives, whether fictive or not, that have been produced for the purpose of *making sense* out of a patchwork of sometimes random, isolated, and often discontinuous events. Yet there appears to be some ambivalence with regard to conveying such knowledge. On the one hand, for many peoples and civilizations, knowledge of the past has been conveyed amongst and through generations in the form of myths, legends, anecdotes, and oral histories, where multiple versions of each event or series of events run parallel to each storyteller's layer of subjectivity. On the other hand, history as a discipline of western thought has promoted the institutionalization of what Jean-François Lyotard calls a *"grand récit,"*[2] an authoritative, official, and "true" account of a nation's past, which has traditionally been considered a source of objective knowledge.

Until recently, the discipline of historical writing—so called "normative history"—has eluded the categorization of subjectivity inherent in narratives, specifically because historians have for long donned the cloak of objectivity by either choosing what Hayden White describes as "non-narrative" or "anti-narrative" forms of discourse (such as annals and chronicles)[3] or by admittedly relating only what were considered "true," accurate, and thus verifiable, "facts": by communicating a representation of the past "as it really was." However, this claim to objectivity has come under intense scrutiny in the last quarter of the twentieth century with the proliferation and consecration of

---

[1] For a comprehensive investigation of the link connecting narrative, identity, and community, see the collection of essays edited by Lewis P. Hinchman and Sandra K. Hinchman, *Memory, Identity, Community: the Idea of Narrative in the Human Sciences.* Albany: State University of N.Y. Press, 1997. Notably, in the introduction the authors posit that "the story of one's individual life depends on the larger stories of the community to which one belongs. That community, in turn, crystallizes around a stock of common memories revivified in stories" (xxiii-xxiv).

[2] Jean-François Lyotard coined the term *"grand récit,"* which has been translated as "metanarrative" but has also been referred to as "grand narrative" or "master narrative." See *The Postmodern Condition: A Report on Knowledge.* Trans. Geoff Bennington and Brian Massumi. Trans. Minneapolis: U of Minnesota P, 1984, reprint 1997.

[3] See White's "The Value of Narrativity in the Representation of Reality" in *Critical Inquiry* 7.1 (1980): 5-27, reprinted in *The Content of the Form: Narrative Discourse and Historical Representation.* Baltimore: John Hopkins UP, 1987, a study of historical narratives, which includes an explanation by the author of the differences among the various genres of history writing.

postmodernism in the social sciences and the humanities.[4] The so-called "narrative turn," which was part of the wider "linguistic turn," marked a shift from what Jerome Bruner has described as the "paradigmatic mode of cognitive functioning"—whose objective was a "formal, mathematical" system of description and explanation" (12)—to a mode of cognition that privileged what he calls "verismilitude" or "lifelikeness" (17). Hence, the wide-ranging influence of postmodernism initiated a transition where *meaningfulness* became more important than *truthfulness*, inasmuch as narrative construction challenged the supremacy of empirical fact.

The idea of a grand narrative as championed by traditional historians has come under attack from two distinct yet complementary perspectives. On the one hand, the deconstruction of language by semiotics has demonstrated texts in general and narratives in particular to be a reconstituted description by someone, i.e. a "narrator," of a sequence of events experienced and retold by distinct characters, thus not only producing multiple layers of subjectivity in the processes of memorization, extraction, and reconstruction, but injecting a dose of fictionality into the stage of reconstitution and narrativization as well.[5] On the other, cultural critics and new historicists have questioned the authority of master narratives by considering other genres as historical writing[6] and have argued that historians, in relating historical events, are subjected to various socio-political forces that influence and mould their work to conform to certain prevailing ideologies. Yet it would seem somehow out of place for the scope of this introduction to attempt either to retrace the ways in which semiotics has deconstructed language and decentered the subject, or to summarize the interdisciplinary debate spurred by the narrative turn,[7] or even to reiterate the

---

[4] The work of Roland Barthes, Jacques Derrida, Michel Foucault, Hayden White and especially Paul Ricoeur has had considerable influence on the way we conceptualize and approach narratives in general and historical texts in particular.

[5] For a more in-depth exploration of the vanishing boundary between fact and fiction in historical narratives, see for example Roland Barthes's "Le Discours de l'Histoire" *Information sur les Sciences Sociales* 6.4 (1967): 65-75, Paul Ricoeur's *Temps et Récit* (3 vols) Paris: Seuil, 1991, and Hayden White's *The Content of the Form: Narrative Discourse and Historical Representation* Baltimore, MD: John Hopkins UP, 1987. For a contemporary debate, we refer the reader to Volume 9, Issue 2 of *Rethinking History* published in June 2005, which contains a number of essays that specifically address this topic.

[6] See for example, "History and Biography: An Editorial Comment" by Alan Munslow in *Rethinking History* 7:1 (2003): 1-11. Munslow considers biography to be a "significant historical genre" wherein the distinction between history and biography operates on different levels of the author's consciousness.

[7] For a detailed account of this debate, see *Critical Inquiry*, Vol. 7, No.1, containing contributions by prominent figures in narrative theory such as Paul Ricoeur, Hayden

new conceptual paradigms instilled by contemporary critical theory. Nevertheless, an overview of the ways in which critical discourse has shaped our approach to narrating the past seems warranted, especially since the negotiation of history and the reconstruction of memory carry a number of theoretical and practical implications that are in direct correlation with the configuration of past events into narrative form.

In parallel to the general state of scepticism towards the master narrative brought forth by postmodernism, feminist studies in particular—and later, cultural studies—have challenged normative history specifically in addressing the patriarchal authorial subjectivity of historical texts, where the relative, symbolic, and discursive importance of women and social "others" has systematically been underrepresented.[8] To that effect, Canning points out that although the intersection between poststructuralism and feminism is a possible site of conflict, one considerable area of agreement between the two lies in "the reformulation of subjectivity as a site of disunity and conflict" (371).

Similarly, drawing from the work of Michel Foucault and the French *École des Annales*, new historicists in the United States rely on the premise that history is prone to the same subjectivity and relativity as literature, i.e. fiction, and thus, every historical narrative is the product of various complex and intricate discourses between social, economical, political and cultural forces. In other words, a historical text does not present a thoroughly truthful or strictly objective account of history, but rather, it is the attempt by an author—thus labeled "historian"—to makes sense of a series of historical events by moulding them into a plausible story to produce meaning, a process that Hayden White has dubbed "emplotment."[9]

But while cultural critics and new historicists consider Foucault's work more specifically as it revolves around the discourse of subject, agency, power and knowledge, his contribution to psychotherapy and his discussion on historiography are equally important. *Madness and Civilization*, *The Birth of the Clinic* and *Discipline and Punish* have all had considerable influence on the

---

White, and Robert Scholes.

[8] See for example, Ralph Cohen's "Generating Literary Histories" in *New Historical Study* edited by Jeffrey N. Cox and Larry J. Reynolds, Princeton: Princeton UP, 1993 for a concise overview or Joan W. Scott's "The Evidence of Experience" in *Critical Inquiry* 17 (1991): 773-797 for a specific case study on the ways in which the challenge to normative history has been brought forth by texts of social others, and how such texts historicize their otherness and their difference.

[9] White apparently coined the term in "The Historical Text as Literary Artifact" printed in *Tropics of Discourse: Essays in Cultural Criticism*, Baltimore: John Hopkins UP, 1978, which, according to the endnote, is a revised version of a lecture given before the Comparative Literature Colloquium of Yale University on January 24, 1974.

field of narrative therapy, as psychoanalysts [10] have adapted Foucault's conceptualization of systems of thought as institutions of power to the extent that one's sense of exclusion in a community (e.g. the marginalized member of a family) can be mediated by the inclusion of the person's story within the dominant narrative that has shaped that community. Through the deconstruction of the various processes that lead to the establishment of *discursive formations* and their emerging disciplines in *Archaeology of Knowledge*, Foucault questions the view that these formations are constructed around unified and continuous discourses. Rather, he believes that these discursive events, which are sporadic, isolated, and dispersed in their manifestation, are only assembled through an intricate web of connections and interchanges. Foucault's explanation of his methodology, his "archaeology," and the concurrent demystification of the tenets of continuity and unity, bring forth a perspective that runs against the grain of traditional historiography and "normative" history which consider historical writing to be cohesive and objective.

Perhaps more significantly, structuralists and poststructuralists have been most active in voicing widespread scepticism towards both the authority and the assumed objectivity of History by claiming that the very structure of narrative is *de facto* a construction, i.e. a "fabrication," by someone for somebody, and that hence, in such a process, a certain degree of fictionality and subjectivity is unavoidable. A brief reminder of the basic conceptual implications of the phenomenology of experience, memorization, extraction, and communication would not only allow us to understand this claim but also to attempt to grasp the theoretical and practical consequences of narrativization.

As events are *witnessed* or *experienced* by various people, passive or active participants, they are stored as a particular and personalized image and/or impression in their individual and/or collective memory, [11] through an unconscious process of internalization. To be transcribed into intelligible form to be communicated, shared, and understood, these events (or their corresponding images and impressions) are collected or extracted from each individual and/or collective memory ("rememorized") before being reconstructed.[12] They are then codified into common language in the form of

---

[10] Psychoanalyst Michael White has drawn extensively from the work of Foucault and other poststructuralists such as Jacques Derrida in his seminal article, "Deconstruction and Therapy," in which he describes the narrative approach to therapy which has gained widespread popularity amongst family therapists.

[11] In *Mémoire, Histoire, Oubli* Paul Ricoeur suggested that there is some tension regarding the intersection between the public/private and collective/individual properties of memory.

[12] Ricoeur has also pointed out that memory can either be stored as a vivid image or dwell in one's unconscious until it is reenacted through a conscious process of extraction.

statements and sentences—marking textually the existence of actors, their actions, and their consequences: subjects, verbs, objects. Consequently, these statements are organized into a *sequence*—it is this particular sequencing of events that constitutes "narrativizing," i.e. shaping events into narrative form— according to various organizing principles before adopting the shape of paragraphs, series of paragraphs, and text.

The configuring of events into a narrative structure is what poststructuralists consider to be the construction of a plot—i.e. emplotment—a process that confers symbolic or factual meaning to a succession of events and which closely replicates the structural foundation of a story, whether imaginary or real. To that effect, Paul Ricoeur explains how the gap between events and story is bridged by the concept of plot:

> By plot I mean the intelligible whole that governs a succession of events in any story. This provisory definition immediately shows the plot's connecting function between an event or events and the story. A story is *made out of* events to the extent that plot *makes* events *into* a story. ("Narrative Time" 171)

In broader terms perhaps, a narrative is a story insofar as it contains distinctive protagonists (*who*), actions (*what*), and a plot (*who* does *what, how* and possibly *why*), and a beginning, middle, and end. From this perspective, then, it is easy to understand that since there is a multitude of ways of sequencing events, there is consequently a multitude of narratives: "It is a commonplace of modern relativism," W.J.T Mitchell observes, "that there are multiple versions of events and the stories about them and that there is something suspect about claims to having the 'true' or 'authorized' or 'basic' version in one's possession" (2).

The Historian's work, then, not only demands both the reconstruction of memory and a renegotiation of the past generated by the task of unearthing a wide variety of sources (such as personal and collective memories, archives, literature), and compiling them alongside an already existing body of work, but also their (re)structuring: the sequencing and ordering of the events depicted in this body of work through narrativization. It is through this very process that meaning is conveyed to the reader—to make sense of real events, events that, in their sporadic and isolated manifestation, do not necessarily follow an organizing principle; as White suggested, the push towards narrativization "arises out of a desire to have real events display the coherence, integrity, fullness, and closure of an image of life that is and can only be imaginary" ("Value" 27).

More specifically, in narrating the past, the *historian*—or *author* who coincidentally also becomes the *narrator* or even perhaps the *storyteller*—selectively remembers and/or collects and selects—whether consciously or unconsciously—events or their statements (such as anecdotes, texts, records) related to or revolving around a specific culture or community. These selected events and the "relative reality" they represent are then organized, i.e. put into a *sequence*, according to a number of organizing principles such as chronological order or level of importance (for that given culture or community). Of particular interest within the process of selection and categorization in the transcription of past events is the unavoidable presence of the narrator's subjectivity in transcribing these events not only through the possibilities offered by the organizing principle but also by the various stages of the process outlined above. This is particularly accurate from the onset of the process if we consider that events, or in this case "historical facts" (which, one assumes, are based on "reality" [13]), are built upon experience, then the subjectivity of such experiences (whether from the person experiencing it or the historian recounting it) is unavoidable.

The classical historicist claim to objectivity falters in the face of the aforementioned claims. On the one hand, feminism and cultural studies have enlightened our reading of normative history by unveiling subjective ideologies of exclusion and discrimination and by drawing our attention to texts of social others that have been suppressed as a result of these ideologies. On the other hand, studies in the phenomenology of memorization and narrativity have not only revealed the subtleties of fictionality in history writing but also questioned the objectivity of historical writing. As Paul Ricoeur has pointed out, there are always two central questions in his phenomenology of memory: "de quoi *y a-t-il souvenir?* de qui *est la mémoire?*" (*La mémoire* 3). This view with regard to the inherent subjectivity of narratives parallels Scholes' observation that "Narrative is not just a sequencing ... narrative is a sequencing of something for somebody" (209).

It was with these questions in mind that we planned the Fall 2005 conference of the CEA-CC, hoping to receive a dialogue that would address the key issues related to the ways in which narratives, both personal and collective, fictional and historical, literary as well as visual, are shaped and created, told and retold, read and reread, grasped, understood, and reassessed by authors and audiences, past and present, in a wide variety of contexts. Considering key theoretical issues and addressing three distinct yet intersecting discourses—the boundary between fact and fiction, the influence of postcolonial literature and

---

[13] This apposition would be refuted by Roland Barthes, however, who argued that "facts" only exist linguistically: *le fait n'a jamais qu'une existence linguisitique* (73) in "Le Discours de l'Histoire" *Information sur les Sciences Sociales* 6.4 (1967): 65-75.

theory on world history in general and the Caribbean in particular, and the challenges posed by feminism to normative history—the contributions to this volume offer an eclectic array of case studies at the crossroads of narrativity and history.

Paralleling the debate addressing the literality of history, liberal humanistic studies have always regarded literary texts to be representative of distinct periods of history and have considered that, to some extent, the work of some authors resembles that of a historian. As suggested earlier, perhaps the most central issue regarding narratives, whether historical, fictional, or biographical, has revolved around what can be regarded as "fact"—what is/was "real"—and what can be considered "fiction"—what "imaginary" elements have been woven in or added by the author. At one end of the spectrum, beyond the need to transcribe events into meaningful form, historians have always relied on fictional elements to provide continuity and comply with the ideological and stylistic canons of history writing. On the other, authors of fiction very often rely on certain geographical, political, historical, and/or cultural elements, injecting a dose of fact, e.g. "reality," into their texts to create a distinct space of temporal and spatial liminality, and thus becoming themselves subjects of the specific context from which they draw their inspiration. Although there seems to be some amount of debate among scholars with regard to the perception of falsehood that accompanies the fictionality of historical narrative, [14] the distinction between history and fiction, as Robert Scholes has pointed out, principally rests on the assumption that in history proper the events described did occur (in "reality") before the text—history is then, as commented above, a "selective" representation, whereas in a work of fiction the events are created for and within the text (211).

Consequently, a number of papers at the conference specifically addressed the intersection of fact and fiction that narrative addresses. Mary Leonard's essay engages with the work of writers such as V.S. Naipaul, Salman Rushdie, Yann Martell, and Ian McEwan in order to assess the ways in which fiction and nonfiction are used to explore, illustrate and/or represent the turbulent history of our world. In particular, the essay takes as its starting point Naipaul's assertion that the novel is a dead form because the world has lost interest in fiction. While some authors may indeed argue that at the dawn of the twenty-first century history (i.e. fact) has by far exceeded the imaginary (i.e. fiction), others claim

---

[14] See for example, Stephen Carr's "History, Fiction, and Human Time" and "Narrative and the Real World: an Argument for Continuity," in which the author responds to poststructuralstm's scepticism towards the aptitude for historical writing accurately to represent the past "as it really was." In opposition to the concept that historical narratives are pure fabrications, Carr posits that narrative structures form an inherent part of reality as it is experienced and represented.

that fictive literature remains an important narrative genre. Leonard contends that the fictional narrative is not dying but "evolving." On a different level, Darrell Fike's contribution combines the two ("fact" and "fiction") by using both creative and critical prose to explore the shared border of the remembered world and the dreamed world. Echoing observations made earlier regarding the properties of recollecting, Fike notes that while "remembering" can be characterized as an activity of the conscious mind to recall empirically provable events, it shares many psychic qualities with a principal function of the unconscious mind—that of dreaming. Memory, when viewed from this perspective, can be seen as a psychic construction that comes into being not purely as an artifact of the outside world but as a function of the interior world that serves as the site of its creation, existence, and retrieval. The discourse connecting Truth, Fiction, History, and Memory is also addressed through an investigation of literary texts. Christopher Powers' paper analyzes Toni Morrison's novels *Beloved, Jazz,* and *Paradise* to investigate Morrison's "spatialization of time," arguing that "Morrison does not spatialize time with the purpose of undoing master narratives" but "because it is part of her innovation as a writer to show how people experience memory synchronically." Powers stresses that the political reading reproduces "a stigma long attached to African American writers, who are presumed to be more political because they are African American." In "Truth versus Knowledge: (Re)Interpreting the Traumatic Memory of Chappaquiddick in Joyce Carol Oates' *Black Water,*" Matthew O. Cleveland retraces the incident that occurred at Chappaquiddick, Massachusetts on the night of July 18, 1969, when Senator Edward Kennedy drove off a wooden bridge in an accident that caused the drowning death of his passenger, 28-year-old Mary Jo Kopechne, as it is told in Oates' novella. Using Jean Laplanche's elaboration of Freud's concept of *Nachträglichkeit* (which Laplanche terms 'afterwardsness') dialectically with Lacan's conceptual dichotomy between Truth and Knowledge, Cleveland's essay demonstrates that the author's *interpretation* of the traumatic (historic) incident at Chappaquiddick enacts an hystericized discourse that in turn reveals important Truths about individual and collective desire beyond the 'objective' (and objectifying) versions of the incident provided by Kennedy and other 'official' sources. While this discussion might accurately illustrate the debate regarding the oppositional binary of fact and fiction as it pertains to historical writing, as W.J.T. Mitchell has pointed out, "the real problem, however, is not the telling of true stories from false … but the very value of narrativity as a mode of making sense of reality (whether the factual reality of actual events, or the moral, symbolic reality of fictions)" (2).

- As perhaps the most prominent figure in cultural studies, the late Edward Said reminded us of the crucial role played by postcolonial literature in the (re)affirmation of "otherness" not only within the social sciences but within the context of world history as well:

> ... in the decades-long struggle to achieve decolonisation and independence from European control, literature has played a crucial role in the re-establishment of a national cultural heritage, in the re-instatement of native idioms, in the re-imagining and re-figuring of local histories, geographies, communities. (1)

This reimagining has been of particular importance in the history of the Caribbean, whose legacy of slavery, genocide, colonization, and diaspora is interwoven with its art and culture. In response to V. S. Naipaul's assertion that culture was "mimicry" and history "dead" in the Caribbean, Derek Walcott famously argued:

> In the Caribbean history is irrelevant, not because it is not being created, or because it was sordid; but because it has never mattered. What has mattered is the loss of history, the amnesia of the races, what has become necessary is imagination, imagination as necessity, as invention. (6)

Addressing the issue of the necessity of imagination in the telling of Caribbean history, Robert Miltner investigates the work of poet Rane Arroyo who explores his Puerto Rican heritage in the poetry sequence *Hungry Ghost* in which he, as poet, engages in dialogue with the historical figure of Ponce de León rather than with grand narratives. In his essay "Masks, Mirrors, Mirth and Memory in Rane Arroyo's *Hungry Ghost: The Ponce de León Poems*," Miltner argues that in the process, "Arroyo learns to confess the scars of history, of blood, of hunger, and finally, his need for 'an honest ghost' to aid him, even if that ghost is de León." The confluence between loss and amnesia in the Caribbean is also addressed by Jocelyn A. Géliga Vargas in an essay that examines the reconstruction of Puerto Rican historiography as projected in Noel Quiñones' 1986 documentary *Raíces Eternas*. By exploring the various views on the relationship between history and film–some seeing documentary as evidence, others as didactic, and still others as a reconstruction of the past–Géliga Vargas sees documentary film as "not just a purveyor of history but also an intervention in the making of history," and contends that *Raíces Eternas* is a "project as well as a projection of Puerto Rican history." She posits that while the film was/is considered by many to be a faithful reconstruction of Puerto Rico's history, it contains numerous ruptures that put into question its actual validity as historical document. At a slightly different latitude, Tatiana Tagirova's essay retraces the world travels of Jamaican-born Claude McKay from the perspective of his reception in Russia, arguing that as his national and international consciousness grew as a result of his travels within the United States, England, Russia, Germany, France, Spain, and Morocco, his awareness of social injustices and inequalities also increased.

Earlier, we noted that the narrative turn brought forth by poststructuralism had a far-reaching interdisciplinary impact. Don Walicek's "Stories that Save Themselves: Notes on Fieldwork in Anguilla" questions the tendency in sociolinguistics to "relegate the 'non-linguistic' and personal narratives to the margins." His essay unites the "personal" with the "scientific" to combine a set of personal stories and recollection with data from interviews with Anguillian "culture-bearers," thus explaining the shift of his "attention from the analysis of synchronic phenomena to the relationship between processes of language- and history-making." In doing so, Walicek draws from the conceptual frameworks of James Clifford and Roy Harris, which link history-making with language-making, to go beyond "empiric" data and offer an account of Anguilla's past in which personal narratives are not relegated to the margins, but centered, re-told and re-created, focusing especially on "the role the anecdotal can play" in comprehending the breadth of the processes by which "Anguillian and the social identities of its speakers are constructed." As Walicek's essay illustrates, "Stories populating lived experience serve as a reminder that taxonomic systems, like representations of the past, are constituted in use."

As noted previously, at their intersection with postmodernism, feminist studies were instrumental in decentering the western patriarchal subject alongside, or perhaps even preceding, cultural studies. Considering the female subject with regard to classical texts, Nick Haydock offers an intertextual reading of the stories of Troy by Homer, Chaucer, and Robert Henryson at the crossroads of feminism and postmodernism in his essay "Preposterous Women: The Truth of History and the Truth about Women in Ancient and Medieval Troy Narratives." Examining the influence and portrayal of women with regard to artistic production from Antiquity to Modernity, Haydock argues that "the debasement of women in Troy narratives is repeatedly allied with failures of artistic control, incomplete revision, and especially with false, incongruous supplements." Proceeding to stories actually told by women, Dorsia Smith and Libe García Zarranz examine the narratives of women by focusing on the intersection of gender and oppression in diaspora texts by women: Haitian-born Edwidge Danticat (who now lives in the US) and Merlinda Bobis (a Filipino-Australian writer), respectively. Smith's essay focuses on Danticat's novels *Breath, Eyes, Memory* and *The Dew Breaker*, which through the memories of their protagonists take the reader to Haiti during the time of the corrupt rule of Haiti's President François "Papa Doc" Duvalier from 1964-1971 and the feared *Tonton Macoutes* policemen. Her essay investigates the ways in which the violent history of Haiti during Duvalier's rule is reconstructed and re-told 's novels, by drawing attention more particularly to the mental se suffered by women at the hands of the Macoutes. From the rative therapy, Danticat's narratives parallel stories that aim to iological wounds of the traumatized subject through the of such traumas. García Zarranz's "Tales of Sound and Fury: inda Bobis's *White Turtle*" analyzes the complex significance female characters portrayed in Merlinda Bobis's short-story *Turtle* set in the South Pacific. In particular, her study focuses ues–sexuality and identity–which enable us to concentrate on spects such as motherhood, power structures, the role of silence, ruction of a "displaced" self, thus encapsulating Lewis P. Hinchman and Sandra K. Hinchman's claim that "narrative ... emphasizes the active, self-shaping quality of human thought, the power of stories to create and refashion personal identity" (xiv). In a sense, Bobis's stories may well be seen as counterstories, or "narratives of resistance" to use Hilde Lindemann Nelson's definition[15], stories that aim to re-position the marginalized other by challenging the prevailing hegemonic narrative.

Terry Eagleton recently announced the "Death of Theory" and while the twenty-first century might have claimed the lives of some of its remaining celebrated figures (such as Jacques Derrida and Edward Said), it is undeniable that their legacy is alive and well. The postmodern era has witnessed the promulgation of a multitude of critical approaches, each distinctive in its own way yet at the same time intersecting one another. Hinchman and Hinchman might differentiate theory and narrative by noting that "narrativists usually conceive theories as attempts to capture and elaborate some timeless, essential reality 'behind' the world of human events, whereas narratives undertake the more modest task of organizing and rendering meaningful the experiences of the narrator in that world" (xv). Yet very much like the multiple perspectives represented in the world narratives, these approaches have promoted a plurality of insights into the stories that have shaped our world. Whether biographical or historical, fictive or factual, imaginary or real, these stories are constantly being scrutinized by critics and scholars in order to reconstruct a more comprehensive and perhaps more accurate account of the past; a reconstruction which would possibly allow us better to understand the present and possibly prepare for the future. While the essays in this volume might only represent a sample of the exhaustive studies conducted of the many records that populate the shelves of the world's narratives, they nevertheless strive to reach the same objective. By

---

[15] In "Resistance and Insubordination" *Hypatia* 10.2 (1995): 23-40, Hilde Lindemann Nelson explains that counterstories, which she describes as "narratives of resistance"(24), "are told for the specific purpose for resisting and undermining a dominant story" (34).

deconstructing and reconstructing their subjects from different narratives and theories, these essays unveil the existing ruptures in the form and content of master narratives, which they attempt to mend in order to produce a more inclusive and representative construction of the past, and perhaps at the same time, to create within and out of themselves narratives that more closely resemble the protean nature of what has been considered an unchanging truth.

Works Cited

Bruner, Jerome. *Actual Minds, Possible Worlds.* Cambridge, MA.: Harvard University Press, 1986.

Barthes, Roland. "Le Discours de l'Histoire." *Information sur les Sciences Sociales* 6.4 (1967): 65-75.

Canning, Kathleen. "Feminist History after the Linguistic Turn: Historicizing Discourse and Experience." *Signs* 19.2 (1994): 368-404.

Carr, David. "History, Fiction, and Human Time." *History and the Limits of Interpretation: A Symposium.* <http://cohesion.rice.edu/humanities/csc/conferences.cfm?doc_id=350> n. pg.

—. "Narrative and the Real World: An Argument for Continuity." *History and Theory* 25.2 (1986): 117-131.

Cohen, Ralph. "Generating Literary Histories." *New Historical Study: Essays on Reproducing Texts, Representing History..* Eds. Jeffrey N. Cox and Larry J. Reynolds Princeton: Princeton UP, 1993. 39-53.

Foucault, Michel. *The Archaeology of Knowledge and the Discourse on Language.* A. M. Sheridan Smith trans. New York: Pantheon, 1972.

—. *The Birth of the Clinic: An Archaeology of Medical Perception.* Trans. A. M. Sheridan Smith. New York: Pantheon, and London: Tavistock, 1973.

—. *Discipline and Punish: The Birth of the Prison.* Trans. Alan Sheridan. New York: Pantheon, 1978.

—. *Madness and Civilization: A History of Insanity in the Age of Reason.* Trans. Richard Howard. New York: Pantheon, 1965.

Hinchman, Lewis P. and Sandra K. Hinchman, eds. *Memory. Identity, Community: the Idea of Narrative in the Human Sciences.* Albany: State University of N.Y. Press, 1997.

Lyotard, Jean-François. *The Postmodern Condition: A Report on Knowledge.* Trans. Geoff Bennington and Brian Massumi. Minneapolis: U of Minnesota P, 1984, reprint 1997.

Mink, Louis. "Everyman his or her own Annalist." *Critical Inquiry* 7.1 (1980): 777-783.

Mitchell, W. J. T. "Editor's Note: On Narrative." *Critical Inquiry* 7.1 (1980): 1-4.

Munslow, Alan. "History and Biography: An Editorial Comment." *Rethinking History* 7.1 (2003): 1-11.

Nelson, Hilde Lindemann. *Damaged Identities: Narrative Repair.* Ithaca & London: Cornell University Press, 2001.

Newton, Lowder Judith. "History as Usual? Feminism and the New Historicism." *The New Historicism.* Ed. H. Aram Veeser. New York: Routledge, 1989. 152-167.

Parry, Alan and Robert E. Doan. *Story Re-Visions: Narrative Therapy in the Postmodern World.* New York: Guilford Press, 1994.

Rabine, Leslie Wahl. "A Feminist Politics of Non-Identity." *Feminist Studies* 14.1 (1988): 10-31.

Ricoeur, Paul. *La Mémoire, L'Histoire, L'Oubli.* Paris: Éditions du Seuil, 2000.

—. "Narrative Time." *Critical Inquiry* 7.1 (1980): 169-190

—. *Temps et Récit* (3 vols) Paris: Éditions du Seuil, 1991.

Said, Edward W. "Figures, Configurations, Transfigurations." *Race and Class* 32 (1990): 1-16.

Scholes, Robert. "Language, Narrative, and Anti-Narrative." *Critical Inquiry* 7.1 (1980): 204-212.

Scott, Joan W. "The Evidence of Experience." *Critical Inquiry* 17.4 (1991): 773-797.

Walcott, Derek. "The Caribbean: Culture or Mimicry?" *Journal of Interamerican Studies and World Affairs* 16.1 (1974): 3-13.

White, Hayden. *The Content of the Form: Narrative Discourse and Historical Representation.* Baltimore, MD: John Hopkins UP, 1987

—. "The Historical Text as Literary Artifact." *Tropics of Discourse: Essays in Cultural Criticism.* Baltimore and London: John Hopkins University Press, 1985.

—. "The Value of Narrativity in the Representation of Reality." *Critical Inquiry* 7.1 (1980): 5-27.

White, Michael. "Deconstruction and Therapy." *Therapeutic Conversations.* Ed. Stephen Gilligan and Reese Price. New York: Norton, 1993. 22-61.

Williams, Gareth. "The Genesis of Chronic Illness: Narrative Reconstruction," *Sociology of Health and Illness* 6 (1984): 175-200.

Worthington, Kim L. *Self as Narrative: Subjectivity and Community in Contemporary Fiction.* Oxford: Clarendon Press: New York: Oxford University Press, 1996.

Part I

Telling the Past: Between Fact and Fiction

TO NARRATE THE PAST:
THE USES OF FICTION/THE USES OF NONFICTION

MARY LEONARD

According to Steven Connor, cultural changes occurring in Britain after the 1960s created the conditions for a "huge expansion of history and historymaking" in the contemporary British novel (qtd. in Tew 124). This fascination with history was also manifest in the development of British heritage cinema starting in the 1980s. The American historian Eric Foner notes a similar tendency for filmic and literary texts to engage increasingly with history in the United States starting in the 1990s:

> To the surprise of historians themselves, in the final years of the twentieth century and opening moments of the twenty-first, history seemed to enter into Americans' public and private consciousness more powerfully than in any time in recent memory. Our equivalent of what the British call the 'heritage industry' reached unprecedented levels of popularity and profitability. (ix)

Why then, if the above would seem to suggest that fictional forms have been energized by this engagement with history, does V.S. Naipaul, winner of the 2001 Nobel Prize for Literature, insist that the novel is a dead form? His words would appear to suggest that, for Naipaul, it is a 19th-century genre unsuited to the contemporary world:

> We are all overwhelmed by the idea of French 19th-century culture. Everybody wanted to go to Paris to paint or write. And of course that's a dead idea these days...We've changed. The world has changed. The world has grown bigger. (26)

Only by writing nonfiction in this new world, he asserts, is he able to continue to write fiction: "What I felt was, if you spend your life just writing fiction, you are going to falsify your material...and the fictional form was going to force you to do things with the material, to dramatize it in a certain way. I thought nonfiction gave one a chance to explore the world, the other world, the world that one did not know fully...if I didn't have this resource of nonfiction I would have dried up perhaps. I'd have come to the end of my material..." (qtd in

Donadio, "Naipaul" 26). In April of 2005, the British writer Ian McEwan, who has written novels which explore the relationship of the past to the present, also voiced a need to turn to nonfiction in this post-9/11 world where older ideas of the fictional narrative suddenly seemed irrelevant:

> For a while I did find it wearisome to confront invented characters. I wanted to be told about the world. I wanted to be informed. I felt that we had gone through great changes, and now was the time to go back to school, as it were, and start to learn. ("Conversation")

How then *do* we make sense of the turbulent recent history of our world? What are the uses of fiction for such a purpose? What are the uses of nonfiction?

It has been said that the novel helps us know not the news of the headlines but the intimate details of the everyday historical world. It is usually assumed to be a fictional form, though there are, of course, non-fiction novels. Unlike the romance or certain types of poetry, it is not given to flights of fancy, but rather grounds itself in verisimilitude and the mundane. Jane Austen shows us the rituals involved in finding a suitable marriage partner in early 19th-century England, Zola the conditions of the poor in late 19th-century France, Thomas Mann the German evolution from 19th-century humanism to 20th- century decadence. However, as Naipaul asserts, we no longer live in the conditions that produced these novels. Marshall McLuhan has chronicled the rise of the media-saturated age which has supplanted it. Alvin Toffler has diagnosed our Future Shock. Frederic Jameson has lamented the loss of meaning caused by postmodern fragmentation. And Guy DeBord has claimed that the second half of the 20th century has made of us a "society of the spectacle." Trapped in such a hermetic mirror world of simulated realities, composed of an avalanche of seductive imagery and sound bites, is it still possible, or even particularly interesting, to "know" the world in the novelistic sense? Naipaul seems to think not:

> Books require an immense amount of energy. It is not just pages. It is ideas, observations, many narrative lines...I have no faith in the survival of the novel. It is almost over. The world has changed and people do not have the time to give that a book requires. (Atlas 14)

Benjamin Kunkel concurs, "The society of the spectacle has never before reared so high; the novel has never seemed so marginal a form" (14). Like Rushdie, he points to that power which novelists have traditionally enjoyed as social critics, and attributes it largely to an ability to use language, a skill that seems to have lost the importance it once had:

The novelist's command of language, his ability to represent things persuasively, his arbitration of the fates of (imaginary) human beings–all of these resemble actual political power, and probably involve a suppressed wish to wield such power. We can think of the correlation anthropologists have found in many tribal societies between eloquence and authority; we can recall, often with a shudder, various impressive orators of the 20th century; and we can reflect that in the 1960s, both Norman Mailer and Gore Vidal ran for political office. Both lost, but 30 years later would they even have tried? (16)

He concludes that "in modern societies literary power and political power long ago parted ways." If one reflects upon the fact that one of the running jokes about the current American president has to do with his inability to use language accurately and effectively, Kunkel's view would seem to hold true.

The transcendental importance attributed to the "great works of art" that was still prevalent in the first half of the twentieth century would also now seem to be a thing of the past. For a modernist like Djuna Barnes, writing in the 30s, the rich complexity of meaning that can be achieved in artforms like painting or the novel can only be the fruit of a highly developed civilization. As she writes:

the purely happy and contented state of the native, say of Tahiti (before we got in there) was, as Melville found, too damned heavenly and perfect for endurance, we have eaten of the apple,–these peoples have music, dance (I never saw anything more beautiful than the Bal[i]nese dancers at the Paris exposition) and drawing, common to all heathen people, but they did not have books[. T]hey have folk tales, but that, tho[ugh] beautiful is not Shakespeare[;] they have music (and tho[ugh] I am most prone to it) they have no Bach, they have primitive drawings (which I love, in most cases) but they are not Giotto or Veron[e]se, or Carpaccio. Yams fall into their mouth[s], but perfection does not fall into their art complete and total, as it does from these masters. (Letter to Emily Coleman)

Like Naipaul, Guy DeBord suggests that in our increasingly fragmented and mediatized world we no longer have the attention span necessary for the appreciation of such "great art." For him, the problem is not the loss of a particular art form, like the novel, as much as the loss of a unified and meaningful communal life. As he sees it, "Culture is the locus of a search for lost unity" (130), adding, "The greatness of art only begins to fall as dusk begins to fall over life" (133). In other words, the pathos of great art is related to its function of symbolically evoking the traces of a lost plenitude in which creativity was an organic part of the wholeness of communal life, that is, a world that is no longer ours.

Asked how he felt about living in this new kind of world, Marshall McLuhan responded:

I don't like to tell people what I think is good or bad about the social and psychic changes caused by new media, but if you insist on pinning me down about my own subjective reactions as I observe the reprimitivization of our culture, I would have to say that I view such upheavals with total personal dislike and dissatisfaction. I do see the prospect of a rich and creative retribalized society–free of the fragmentation and alienation of the mechanical age–emerging from this traumatic period of culture clash; but I have nothing but distaste for the process of change. As a man molded within the literate Western tradition, I do not personally cheer the dissolution of that tradition through the electric involvement of all the senses: I don't enjoy the destruction of neighborhoods by high-rises or revel in the pain of identity quest. No one could be less enthusiastic about these radical changes than myself. I am not, by temperament or conviction, a revolutionary; I would prefer a stable, changeless environment of modest services and human scale. TV and all the electric media are unraveling the entire fabric of our society, and as a man who is forced by circumstances to live within that society, I do not take delight in its disintegration. ("The Playboy Interview")

It may appear that Naipaul, DeBord, and McLuhan point to an inevitable loss of culture, to the death of literature and, by implication, to a tragic waning of our ability to write–and to read and understand–the collective histories and personal narratives of our culture(s) in the ways we used to. We are less than we were, they may seem to say, we can only lament the substitution of those rich and complex narrative forms by cheap and gaudy forms of spectacle which encourage us in our lazy tendency to abstain from active and informed engagement with the cultures we have created. Rachel Donadio would seem to agree when she claims that fiction does not now, as it did in the past, help us to better understand the world we live in. Despite the fact that escapist fiction, like *Harry Potter* or *The DaVinci Code,* sells well, she asserts, "To date, no work of fiction has perfectly captured our historical moment the way certain novels captured the Gilded Age, or the Weimar Republic, or the cold war" ("Truth," 27), and adds, "The American appetite for experimental fiction does seem pretty small these days" ("Truth," 27).

This does seem to be borne out. In the years after 9/11, nonfiction sales have greatly outstripped fiction sales. Reviews of literary works in the *New York Times* dwindled in comparison with the growing amount of space devoted to works of nonfiction such as journalism and biography. The *9/11 Commission Report* has sold over a million copies. Janet Maslin describes the new books chronicling firsthand experiences of the Iraq war as a veritable "deluge of memoirs" (E1). Elizabeth Becker's 1986 history of modern Cambodia, *When the War Was Over*, and a 1994 Cambodian film based on one of the stories recounted in the book, have been enduring bestsellers in that country. Even serious writers and readers of literature like Naipaul and McEwan are resorting to nonfiction as a means of understanding the world we live in. And magazines that used to publish fiction have been reducing or eliminating the space they allot to it. In August of 2005, Adrienne Miller, a novelist and the literary editor of *Esquire,* summed up the situation:

> We're in a dark cultural moment. I think people seem to feel more comfortable with nonfiction. The tragic theme here is that literary fiction has very limited cultural currency now. Fewer and fewer people seem to believe fiction is still essential for our emotional and intellectual survival. (qtd. in Donadio, "Truth" 27)

But perhaps the message is less about death than it is about change, which sometimes feels like death. As Donadio, thinking about the present moment writes, "It's still early. Nonfiction can keep up with the instant messenger culture. Fiction takes its own sweet time" ("Truth" 27). And, in the interview cited earlier, McLuhan argues, in essence, that we cannot afford to take a pessimistic position about the changes we are now experiencing:

> The world we are living in is not one I would have created on my own drawing board, but it's the one in which I must live, and in which the students I teach must live. If nothing else, I owe it to them to avoid the luxury of moral indignation or the troglodytic security of the ivory tower and to get down into the junk yard of environmental change and steam-shovel my way through to a comprehension of its contents and its lines of force–in order to understand how and why it is metamorphosing man.

Writers may not wield as much power and influence as they did in the past, but literary fiction has not outlived its usefulness. As Salman Rushdie noted in his welcoming remarks to the delegates of the 2005 Pen Club Conference: "In 1986 it still felt natural for writers to claim to be, as Shelley said, 'the unacknowledged legislators of the world,' to believe in the literary art as the proper counterweight to power, and to see literature as a lofty, transnational, transcultural force that could, in Bellow's great formulation, 'open the universe a little more.' Twenty years later, in our dumbed-down, homogenized, frightened culture, under the thumbs of leaders who seem to think of themselves as God's anointed and of power as their divine right, it is harder to make such exalted claims for mere wordsmiths. Harder, but no less necessary" (31). In like fashion, Yann Martell argues in the introduction of his bestselling novel *Life of Pi,* winner of the 2002 Man Booker Prize, that fictional forms like the novel continue to be extremely important since they enable us to imagine the world in a way which helps us transcend the crude or unpleasant realities we may be mired in, a necessary function in a world full of social, political and personal problems which can easily overwhelm and depress us: "If we citizens do not support our artists, then we sacrifice our imagination on the altar of crude reality and we end up believing in nothing and having worthless dreams" (xiv).

In the introduction to his 1999 collection of short stories *Historias atroces*, (Atrocious Stories), the Puerto Rican writer Pedro Cabiya admits, perhaps facetiously, in erudite, contradictory and ludic Spanglish, to having a short attention span, as well as a number of other psychological disorders, which should perhaps disqualify him from being taken seriously as a writer, at least in traditional terms:

> Si las composiciones de esta colección resultan poco entretenidas *in their own right*, a lo mejor pueda encontrárseles algún interés en el hecho de que son artefactos producidos por un individuo diagnosticado con *obsessive compulsive disorder, short attention span syndrome* y caracterizado como *anal retentive*. Y aunque mi doctor añade *hipocondríaco* y *paranoide*, ahí sí que no, porque no me invento yo estas taquicardias y además tengo pruebas incontrovertibles de que soy el objetivo de terroríficas conspiraciones. Ojalá las cosas nunca lleguen a tal punto que hagan decir mi terapeuta: 'No sé cómo no vi los señales.' Este libro es una posible señal de que algo no anda bien, o bien de que algo no andará bien muy pronto. Alábalo que él vive. [1]

The last statement, "Alábalo que él vive," is a play on words. It could be translated as "Praise the Lord!" But, in this context, it can also be understood to refer to the text itself, asserting the value of the bizarre and disturbing short stories which follow, perhaps precisely because of their strange idiosyncrasies. What is important about this statement has little to do with what neuroses Cabiya might or might not have. What is interesting is how the narrative strategies that he and other contemporary writers employ manifest in, sometimes shocking, but highly creative and articulate ways, the maladies of our time that the critics I have cited have been describing. This is not a writer who aspires to the artistic "perfection" Barnes praised in the thirties. In fact, he does not even seem to dare claim these "atrocious" texts as literature. They are merely "artifacts." But neither is he representative of that "dumbed-down world"

---

[1] 15-16. If the compositions in this collection do not turn out to be very entertaining in their own right, you might perhaps find some interest in the fact that they are artifacts produced by an individual who has been diagnosed with obsessive compulsive disorder, short attention span syndrome and characterized as anal retentive. And, even though my doctor adds hypochondriac and paranoid, there yes but no, because I am not inventing those attacks of tachycardia, and what's more, I have incontrovertible proofs that I am the object of horrifying conspiracies. Hopefully, things will never get to the point where they make my therapist say, "I don't know how I missed the signs." This book is a possible sign that something is wrong or that something will go wrong very soon (translation mine).

Rushdie describes. And, if these are the maladies of our age, then these are the texts we must write.

The fictional narrative, I would submit, is not dying. It is, as we pass from one century to the next, evolving. Some, like Cabiya, are writing brief intense narratives for the jittery, fast-moving world we live in. New novels by writers like Ian McEwan, Pat Barker, Kazuo Ishiguro and others are engaging in striking ways with the traumas of our recent post-9/11 past and the insecurities of our continuing present and our uncertain future–September 11, terrorism, violence, the potential dangers of biotechnology–and showing how these experiences are shaping the texture of our brave new world. And the critics of the *New York Times* have returned to pondering the nature of the literature we are now producing. In fact, this paper is written largely in reaction to the conversation taking place in the *Times Book Review* during the second half of the year 2005.

If I have suggested that nonfiction is, by definition, more simplistic or transparent than fiction, I would like to correct that now by showing that nonfiction writers, like Iaian Sinclair, are also writing in new and challenging ways. Like Guy DeBord, Sinclair is a situationist who resists the loss of cultural specificity and of knowledge in our homogenizing age of the spectacle. In his psycho-geography *London Orbital*, he circumnavigates the M25, the highway that encircles London, and investigates the myriad ways in which it has transformed the psychic experience of space of those who live near it and drive on it. American readers sometimes complain that they find the cultural specificity of Sinclair's London references and the complexity of his language difficult to understand, but these are precisely the characteristics that make him the singular writer he is. John Joss praises the way in which Sinclair "pushes the limits of modern word usage" and marvels at how his "world view engages all six senses, back through the history of England and Europe, across the spectrum of human experience: past and present," and *The San Francisco Chronicle* calls him "a prose stylist without peer."[2]

Perhaps we have not yet found the most useful words to describe the ways in which we are now trying to write our recent experiences, and the varied ways we are employing fiction and non-fiction forms to do it. Can we still just call the way we write Postmodernism, or is that too vague for the specificity of textual approaches like the ones I have discussed? Is it still productive to use a term like Postcolonialism? Or, as Ira Raja asked in a recent post on the University of Pennsylvania Call for Papers website, are we "past the post" now?

---

[2] Blurb on the back cover of *London Orbital*.

Works Cited

Atlas, James. "'Magic Seeds': A Passage to India." *New York Times Book Review*. November 28, 2004. Vol. 154. Issue 53047, 14-15.

Barker, Pat. *Double Vision*. New York: Picador, 2003.

Barnes, Djuna. Letter to Emily Coleman, January 10, 1936. Djuna Barnes Archives. McKeldin Library. University of Maryland at College Park.

Becker, Elizabeth. "Minor Characters." *New York Times Book Review*. August 28, 2005. Vol. 154. Issue 53320, 27.

Cabiya, Pedro. *Historias Atroces*. San Juan and Santo Domingo: Isla Negra, 1999.

DeBord, Guy. *The Society of the Spectacle*. Trans. Donald Nicholson Smith. New York: Zone Books, 1995.

Donadio, Rachel. "The Iracible Prophet: V.S. Naipaul at Home." *New York Times Book Review*. August 7, 2005.Vol. 154. Issue 53299, 8-26.

—. "Truth is Stronger Than Fiction." *New York Times Book Review*. August 7, 2005. Vol. 154. Issue 53299, 27.

Foner, Eric. *Who Owns History?: Rethinking the Past in a Changing World*. New York: Hill and Wang, 2002.

Ishiguro, Kazuo. *Never Let Me Go*. London: Faber and Faber, 2005.

Jameson, Frederic. *Postmodernism or The Cultural Logic of Late Capitalism*. Durham: Duke University Press, 1991.

Joss, John. Review of *London Orbital: A Walk Around the M25*. October 5, 2005. <http://www.amazon.com/gp/cdp/member-reviews/A382MBM8 Y7FBR?ie=UTF8&display=public&page=4>.

Kunkel, Benjamin. "Dangerous Characters." *New York Times Book Review*. September 11, 2005. Vol. 154. Issue 53334, 14-6.

Maslin, Janet. "A Sharing of Chaos: 2 Soldiers, Same Iraq." *New York Times*. August 18, 2005. Vol. 154. Issue 53310, E1-E6.

Martell, Yann. *Life of Pi*. New York: Harvest Books, 2003.

McEwan, Ian. "Conversation: McEwan." Transcript of *NewsHour with Jim Lehrer*. April 13, 2005. PBS. Available: www.pbs.org.

McLuhan, Marshall. "The Playboy Interview." *Playboy Magazine*. March 1969. Online. Available: http://heim.ifi.uio.no/~gisle/overload/mcluhan/ pb.html.

Raja, Ira. "CFP: 'Past the Post?': New Literatures in English in a Globalized World" October 5, 2005. <http://cfp.english.upenn.edu/archive/ 2005-08/0199.html >.

Rushdie, Salman. "The Pen and the Sword". *New York Times Book Review*. April 17, 2005. Vol. 154. Issue 53187, 31.

Sinclair, Iaian. *London Orbital: A Walk Around the M25.* London and New
    York: Granta, 2002.
Tew, Phillip. *The Contemporary British Novel.* London and New York:
    Continuum, 2004.

Remember: A History

Darrell Fike

> On the other hand, whatever the techniques
> employed, commentary's only role is to say
> finally, what has silently been articulated
> deep down. It must–and the paradox is ever-
> changing yet inescapable–say, for the first
> time, what has already been said, and repeat
> tirelessly what was, nevertheless, never said.

Michel Foucault, "The Discourse on Language"

Prologue

The role of memory as both the mechanism of recollection and the content of the recollection mimics the character of language as a system of self-referential signs and discursive practices as described by Michel Foucault in *The Archaeology of Knowledge*. For Foucault, understanding how discourse creates what it seeks to describe means "no longer treating discourses as groups of signs (signifying elements referring to contents or representations) but as practices that systematically form the objects of which they speak" (49). Memory, when viewed from this perspective, can be seen as a psychic construction that comes into being not as an artifact of the outside world but as a function of the interior world that serves as the site of its creation, existence, and retrieval.

While "remembering" is characterized as an activity of the conscious mind to recall empirically provable events, it shares many psychic qualities with a principal function of the unconscious mind—that of dreaming. Memory thus can be seen as the psyche twin of somnambulant dreams, with one twin turned to the outer world and the other to the inner world.

This essay explores the shared border of the remembered world and the dreamed world.

I

My earliest memory is of a dream, a dream I first remember waking from when I was a small boy. I told my mother of the dream as she washed my face in the morning light coming through the small window of the kitchen. She smiled and said not to worry—it was only a dream.

In the dream my grandmother–my mother's mother–is walking with me up a hill. The sky is full of large puffy clouds. She holds my hand in hers.

We reach the top and look out. Below my mother is hanging a sheet on a clothesline behind our small redbrick house. Tiny yellow flowers dot the deep clover in the yard. The clean white bed sheets billow in the breeze. I call and wave to my mother but she does not hear me. I look up at my grandmother instead and she pats my head with her hand. I rub my cheek against the loose cotton of her dress. She points to the distant sky as if she sees something there, and I lean out over the edge following her finger.

Then I am falling, falling, tumbling through the air. I can see my grandmother at the top of the cliff watching me fall. Her mouth makes a small smile. I look past her at the puffy clouds. I am not afraid as I fall until I see the flash of the sheets on the clothesline and know that I am about to strike the earth. I close my eyes and wake up.

II

In "What is an Author," Michel Foucault claims writing to be "an interplay of signs arranged less according to its signified content than according to the very nature of the signifier" (198). As the child/parent of discourse, the signifier is seen here to shape the knowledge it seemingly describes. Foucault continues:

> Writing unfolds like a game [jeu] that invariably goes beyond its own rules and transgresses it limits. In writing, the point is not to manifest or exalt the act of writing, nor is it to pin a subject within language; it is rather a question of creating a space into which the writing subject constantly disappears. (198)

To speak or write is to play a game the rules of which require you to break the rules; to speak or write is to disappear. If I break the rules will you still play this game? And if I disappear into this text, will you find me again?

III

My grandmother died from a cerebral hemorrhage in the drunk tank of the Dallas jail in 1962 at age 43, mother of nine, widow of one, ex-wife of another.

Two photographs of her survive: one, a large framed formal portrait of her in a matronly high collar and a single strand of borrowed pearls that she had made at a department store and sent to my mother the Christmas before she died; the other, a small black-and-white 1950's snapshot of her sipping a Hurricane and smoking a Camel at Pat O'Brien's in New Orleans with an unidentified mustachioed man. Drunken and increasingly disorderly since the death of husband two, she was taken to jail after pulling a gun on a neighbor. Thinking she was just sleeping it off, the guards were not alarmed that she lay mumbling and breathing laboredly on the metal fold-down bunk of the drunk tank. "Sweet dreams, sweetheart" the guard is rumored to have said as he turned the key and walked away.

IV

In *Mythologies*, Roland Barthes examines various cultural phenomena and the myths, or secondary discourse systems, which empower them with signification. Barthes' emphasis is how the mythic process adapts complete signs of various kinds and uses them as signifiers in a secondary system of discourse: "We shall therefore take language, discourse, speech, etc., to mean any significant unit or synthesis, whether verbal or visual: a photograph will be a kind of speech for us in the same way as a newspaper article; even objects will become speech, if they mean something" (110). Thus discourse transforms poetically into figures of myth: "Everything, then, can be a myth? Yes, I believe this, for the universe is infinitely fertile in suggestions" (109). And as the universe whispers suggestively into our ears, we become unwitting accomplices of a crime: "Myth is speech stolen and restored; only, speech which is restored is no longer quite that which is stolen: when it was brought back, it was not put exactly in its place" (125).

V

A kind man named Frank, who had secretly loved my grandmother for years as she served him coffee at the diner where she worked, paid for her funeral when the county threatened to bury her in the pauper's field. Later he sent a letter to my mother saying that my grandmother was not responsible for her actions those last years; a doctor told him that her brain was pitted and scoured like the surface of the moon, the result of tiny veins exploding as she hung up the wash or made change—nickels, pennies and dimes clinking in her palm—at the diner.

Six months later, my own mother sent me running to our neighbor's house for help after she had fallen to the couch, face cocked and left eye closed, unable to stand anymore. For a few weeks, my mother wandered through the house dragging her left leg behind her and tucking her limp arm into her housecoat; like a game, my brother and I began to mimic her, sliding our cotton-socked feet across the hardwood floor of the front hall until our father caught us and gave us a whipping.

VI

Yury Lotman in his essay "The Text in the Text" proclaims that discourse entangles the greatest and the least, weaving all that we know and all that we have forgotten into a terrible tapestry: "Culture in its entirety may be considered a text–a complexly structured text, divided into a hierarchy of intricately interconnected texts within texts.   To the extent that the word 'text' is etymologically linked to weaving, the term's original sense has been restored" (384).

Perhaps, before our text is drawn piecemeal into other texts, we should let Barthes unravel a thread or two, using his *The Pleasure of the Text* to tweeze our own:

Whenever I attempt to "analyze" a text which has given me pleasure, it is not my "subjectivity" I encounter but my "individuality," the given which makes my body separate from other bodies and appropriates its suffering or its pleasure: it is my body of bliss I encounter. And this body of bliss is also my historical subject; for it is at the conclusion of a very complex process of biographical, historical, sociological, neurotic elements (education, social class, childhood configuration, etc.)…that I write myself as subject at present out of place, arriving too soon or too late… (62).

And there we have it, our body of bliss that is both tablet and pen, that writes and is written upon by memory: unfolding from the spine, nerve and vein weave and tease through tissue, a letter-perfect web articulated in the language of blood, the story of a life the first word and the last retold in each beating of the heart.

VII

My mother's alcoholic and sometimes combative younger sister's left pupil takes up almost all of her iris, leaving only a thin scar of blue; most likely, the doctors say, the result of a minor cerebral incident or two; her sisters, their patience worn as thin and brittle as old bone, say that explains it all: like mother like daughter.

Cluster headaches is what they are called for men; when I feel one fragmenting behind my left eye, throbbing and heavy and sharp, I crawl under the sheets and try to sleep, or paradoxically walk rapidly through the neighborhood scowling and cussing, squinting in pain with each breath, until the headache dissipates or intensifies and I slump to the curb.

Vascular constrictions, the thin blue veins in my temporal lobe tightening into a knot; I worry that on the day when one of them finally–snaps snaps–and my synapses flood with blood, will I have a perfect stroke that takes my speech and sight and movement in a single moment? Or will I be caught in between as so many are, in between this moment and the next moment, as if I were falling but never hitting the earth?

VIII

In "Signature Event Context" Jacques Derrida suggests that one of the fundamental characteristics of writing is its iterability, or that it may be repeated (or must be repeated): "In order for my "written communication" to retain its function as writing, i.e., its readability, it must remain readable despite the absolute disappearance of any receiver, determined in general. My communication must be repeatable–iterable–in the absolute absence of the receiver or of any empirically determinable collectivity of receivers" (1173). So our writing must keep talking, though no one listens, indeed though no one will ever listen. And our writing must talk even if it has lost the wag of the author's tongue to give it voice: "But the sign possesses the characteristic of being readable even if the moment of its production is irrevocably lost and even if I do not know what its alleged author-scriptor consciously intended to say at the moment he wrote it, i.e. abandoned it to its essential drift" (1175).

So writing orphaned of both addresser and addressee, continues to function, must function, or else not be writing. Such an orphan then is ripe for adoption, for grafting onto the family tree of our text or any text: "...by virtue of its essential iterability, a written syntagma can always be detached from the chain in which it is inserted or given without causing it to lose all possibility of functioning, if not all possibility of 'communicating,' precisely" (1175).

Now, what if I place your poem in my essay, and it becomes part of my essay, a supporting branch of my thesis. Is it poem or is it essay? And what if I dream of history, of your life story or someone else's life story? Is it dream or is it history?

IX

My first dream is of a memory, a memory I first dreamed when I was a small boy. In the dream I am outside a window on an upper floor of a tall brick apartment building looking in. The bricks are barely yellow and very worn. Inside the room an old man with white hair is sitting in a well-used and comfortable looking armchair. A reading lamp glows beside the chair with a soft candle-like light. The room is quiet and neat. On a small table beside the chair are a photograph in a silver frame and a silent clock. The rest of the room disappears into shadow.

The old man holds a newspaper open and is reading. He is wearing a white undershirt, loose cotton pants, and slippers. His eyes move slowly back and forth as he reads. The left corner of his mouth tugs slightly downward as he turns the page.

Suddenly, the newspaper flutters to the floor and the old man looks up at the window as if he has seen or heard something outside. In that instant, I realize that I am now looking out the window from the inside of the room. I go to the window and lean out into the still air. There is nothing there but the sky and puffy white clouds. I wake up and remember.

Works Cited

Barthes, Roland. "The Death of the Author." *Modern Criticism and Theory.* Ed. David Lodge. New York: Longman, 1988. 167-172.

—. *Mythologies.* New York: Farrar, Straus & Giroux, 1972.

—. The Pleasure of the Text. Trans. Richard Miller. New York: Noonday Press, 1975.

Derrida, Jacques. "Signature Event Context." *The Rhetorical Tradition.* Eds. Patricia Bizzell and Bruce Herzberg. Boston: St. Martin's, 1990. 1168-1184.

Foucault, Michel. *The Archaeology of Knowledge.* Trans. A.M. Sheridan Smith. New York: Pantheon, 1972.

—. "The Discourse on Language." *The Archaeology of Knowledge.* Trans. A.M. Sheridan Smith. New York: Pantheon, 1972. 215-237.

Lotman, Yury M. "The Text in the Text." Trans. Jerry Leo and Amy Madelker. *PMLA* 109 (1994): 377-384.

THE THIRD EYE: LOVE, MEMORY, AND HISTORY IN TONI MORRISON'S *BELOVED, JAZZ* AND *PARADISE*

CHRISTOPHER POWERS

Narration in the novels of Toni Morrison–always complex, never alike from one to another, abundant with unpredictable jumps in time and ruptured recalling–produces a temporality both protean and conscientiously productive of a singular epistemological directedness toward the past. Through an exercise in reading of themes and technical problems in three of Morrison's novels, *Beloved, Jazz* and *Paradise*–which the author herself has said she intended as a trilogy– this intervention aims to shed light on this temporality and on the relation between history, memory and narration in her writing in general. As part of this exercise I will reflect on the unity of the trilogy as a trilogy, which is by no means perspicuous, and engage a specific textual moment from the novel *Paradise* to discuss the stylistic issue of characterization in Morrison's writing, one of the richest aspects of her novels from *The Bluest Eye* to *Love*. The *Beloved/Jazz/Paradise* trilogy performs a reorientation to the problem of history and memory in systematic fashion. Memory, or "rememory" as the character Sethe from *Beloved* calls it (191), enters the novels in a highly determined manner throughout the three novels that both invokes problems of historical narration and impacts on questions of literary style. While incessantly freighted in the critical literature with political overdeterminations, Morrison's writing of the past incorporates and goes beyond a shift toward the African American, feminine subject, to produce important innovations in narrative structure and style. This essay addresses the following questions: What does Morrison's invention of a new novelistic approach to memory, narration, and the past do to her style? How does Morrison's storytelling not just reflect but also perform a new epistemology of the past, the past as such and the utterly singular modern history of African Americans?

The novel *Beloved* can be fruitfully read alongside books like Margaret Walker's *Jubilee* or Sherley Anne William's *Dessa Rose*, novels from the sixties or seventies written in the wake of a shift in the historiography of slavery and African American history in general–that is, these are modern historical novels about slavery written from the perspective of the slave, often informed by the resources offered by the newly developed methods of oral history. The shift provides the template through which the historical consciousness in *Beloved* and the other two novels in the trilogy becomes legible. Each novel in the trilogy provides a subjective reorientation, a new epistemology for pivotal phases or moments of the post-emancipation African American historical trajectory, which I will provisionally mark as 1) Reconstruction, 2) the Great Migration and 3) the civil rights movement era, which *Beloved, Jazz* and *Paradise* deal with respectively. Her historical portraiture of these phases reflects an attention to the perspective of subaltern subjects in the historiography of the African American experience in the wake of the civil rights movement and the impact of Black consciousness on academic thinking from the nineteen-sixties onward, but it does this only in the most oblique and least "historiographical" of voices. This obliqueness makes the historical chronicling in the trilogy both experientially rich and precisely available for a literary-critical reading.

The trilogy not only incorporates the shift in historiography, but performs and enacts its consequences for the most private and profound of subjective experiences, love. Morrison has herself mentioned in a 1998 interview (Rose) that *Beloved, Jazz,* and *Paradise* each deal with different forms of love and their excesses. These correspond to the three Greek words for love: *Beloved* is concerned with *filia*, familial and fraternal love, *Jazz* with *eros* or romantic and sexual love and *Paradise* with *agape*, love of god, subjective and objective genitive. Thus one can identify the unity of the trilogy as the successive fictional historiography of Reconstruction, the Great Migration and the civil rights Era filtered through the lens of the subjective experience of love. The trilogy aims to present a historicized epistemology of love in post-Emancipation African American experience.

Beloved begins on the cusp of emancipation. The story itself is positioned on the historical border between slavery and freedom, memorably symbolized in the scene of the birth of the character Denver, on a rowboat just inside the Ohio River, the dividing line between the south and north. It charts the failure and endurance of love in conditions of slavery and the ambivalent freedom that ensued in the wake of emancipation, through the stories of characters constantly coping with the loss and sometimes recovery of loved ones. *Jazz* is set in 1923 New York, called simply the City, and aims to capture the decade's claims toward and on an optimistically framed future, felt in jazz music and the innovation of the Harlem Renaissance, as well as the violence of rapid change, reflected in a story of passionate love and murder amongst migrants from the South to the North. *Paradise*, the most expansive, magisterial and complex of all Morrison's novels in my opinion, deals primarily with the decades from the fifties to the bicentennial year 1776 in an all-black Southwestern town that registers microcosmically the throes of change and the generational conflict produced by the civil rights movement, in which Old and New Testament concepts of love are tested, played out and contrasted.

Beloved charts the heroic, beleaguered, sometimes desperate, life-or-death attempt to hold together a family through love in the wake of that so-called "peculiar institution" that systematically tore the family structure apart and tried to destroy the very capacity for familial love itself for 400 years, with brute efficiency and the entire force of a baroque legal codification and the fanatically elaborated ideological apparatus that justified slavery and engendered modern racism. *Jazz* subjects its characters, living under the pressures of that racism, to the conflicts that romantic love encounters when confronted with the clash of rural and urban, the aging and the youth, North and South, and rationality and irrationality amongst newly arrived Southern immigrants to the Northern city. The idea of divine love in *Paradise* is framed by the conflict of the religiously defined values of an older generation in a strictly observant, tightly-knit, outwardly pious all-black community with a younger generation influenced by the non-violent, New Testament-inspired values of the civil-rights movement and the emerging feminist and sexual liberation movements.

In chronicling the historical experience of love, Morrison employs a series of genial literary devices and techniques which have provoked much critical discussion in scholarship. Prominent among these is the constant fast-forwarding and rewinding of the temporal setting through flashbacks and stories of the past related by characters or through the meandering, history-purveying eye of an omniscient narrator. Rather than a chronological, diachronic storyline that weaves the evidence of the past into an ordered, *de facto* meaningful narrative, time in Morrison synchronizes various pasts into one level narrative space, which in turn is subjected more to the demands of characterization than to those of narration. This synchronization of narrative, or to put it another way, this spatialization of time, clearly implies a shift away from a linear, teleological narrative and the historical ontologies that such a perspective implies. This is often (correctly) cited as an aspect of Morrison's postmodernism. But the question engenders another problem worth considering. The critical literature on Toni Morrison often reduces the problem of narrative spatialization in Morrison's writing to its metanarratological function in order to render its politics more discursively accessible. In other words, the argument goes, the fracturing of linear narrative in Morrison implies the critique of a hegemonic master narrative that social movements and academics alike promote, a project which I also wholeheartedly endorse. But what is striking is that the importance of narrative spatialization as a literary device is in the first instance that of a writerly problem that has to do with compositional issues of characterization, which is also, I believe, where the first instance of a critical reading should begin. That is to say, Morrison creates characters whose consciousness of time is in fact spatialized, because it is part of her innovation as a writer to show how people experience memory synchronically. Morrison does not spatialize time with the purpose of undoing master narratives, even though this is an effect of it scholars can address, describe, and elucidate through criticism. If one peremptorily circumvents the implications of spatialization for characterization however, one does an injustice to the interpretation and appreciation of these complex literary artifacts. The tendency of Morrison criticism is to downplay the literariness of her production in favor of a historizing reading that stresses the political-ideological importance of her intervention, reproducing a stigma long attached to African American writers, who are presumed to be more political because they are African American. By linking spatialization to characterization I want to turn the focus to literary strategies and techniques that Morrison genially employs to simulate subjective experience, to consider the subject epistemologies constructed, enacted and implied in her novels. And indeed, in these consist, aesthetically and emotionally, the most rewarding aspects of reading Toni Morrison's novels.

I use the word "experience" pointedly, because Morrison writes of subjects, and the moniker of "historical novel" almost shouldn't be applied to her because of the glib objectification common to what today are considered historical novels. Her emphasis on the subjective has produced such unforgettable personalities like Son from *Tar Baby* or Denver from *Beloved*, whose singularity makes them memorable as individuals, even as their experience registers general trends, epochs and movements. One rarely sees dates, important figures, or milestone events mentioned in her novels. Morrison will never write a story *about* Nat Turner's rebellion, Marcus Garvey, the Tulsa race riot, or Rosa Parks, although all of the above resonate through her work. In Morrison we see history and historical things through characters, who always turn out to be both very mundane and very interesting and complex.

Characterization in the trilogy *Beloved/Jazz/Paradise*, however, undergoes a curious process of flattening. Sethe, Paul D., Denver, and Beloved in the novel *Beloved* enjoy Morrison's trademark crisp, high-definition characterization by the flexibly omniscient narrator (similar to that of the characters in *Tar Baby*, which was written right before *Beloved* and which in my view marks the real innovatory shift in her career to the mature style of the trilogy). Characterization of the principal protagonists in *Jazz*, Dorcas, Violet and Joe Trace, recedes somewhat behind or remains in many instances at least obscured by the antics of an unpredictable, unreliable, and showy if unnamed and unidentified first person narrator, through which the novel structurally simulates the principle of improvisation in jazz music. In *Paradise,* the (appropriately) fully omniscient narrator erases altogether the distinction of principals and auxiliaries, multiplying characters copiously and paying each equal attention in constellatory fashion, corresponding to the novel's focus on the collective history of the town Ruby and the so-called Convent itself. Characterization in the trilogy, in effect, seems to follow an amplification of perspective that itself reflects an increasing awareness of a collective African American historical trajectory.

In one passage in the novel *Paradise* (93-100), Steward Morgan, the most powerful, staunchly proud, and protective citizen of the town called Ruby, has a long reverie, in 1973, of the founding, in 1889 or 90, of Haven, the original town from which Ruby sprang. Steward is one of twin brothers and the leader of the attack on the women of the Convent (in 1976) with which the book begins and closes. In the middle of the night Steward can't sleep because his wife is not with him, having chosen to sleep in their other house. He goes horseback riding in the pastures, during which he has a long memory of the stories of his ancestors about the founding of Haven. His "rememory" (to speak with Sethe) is prefaced with a stream of consciousness review of his feelings of devotion to his wife, his dislike of the liberal, tolerant views of the young minister, Misner, from out of town, his disgust with the "cut me some slack" (93) attitude of the youth to which he contrasts the hard-working diligence of the men of his generation, and his proud recollection of a relative's resistance to an incident of racial harassment. This is the first extended scene in which we see Steward alone, without his twin brother Deek, with whom he is identical in seemingly every respect, and we are privy to his thoughts, precisely through his memories. It is a crucial moment in his characterization, which in turn will become central to the culmination of the novel. His long reverie of the original migration of the so-called "8-rock" blooded free African Americans from Louisiana who wander through the post-Reconstruction South to found a new city in Oklahoma is a semi-mythical account of autochthonous origin, the trials of an exodus including the magical appearance of an ancestor who leads the way, and the arrival and settlement at a new, promised land. The recollection combines the delineation of his character with the founding myth of Ruby and the moment when the origin of a central symbol is explained, the tall communal oven which the new settlers erect in the middle of the town and onto which they place a plaque with mysterious words. Partially effaced in the late-forties resettlement of the people of Haven to create the new town of Ruby, the inscription either reads "Beware the furrow of his brow," which is the interpretation of the older generation or "Be the furrow of his brow," the interpretation of the youth (93). The debate over the inscription becomes the focal point of generational conflict.

What is at stake in this scene is at least twofold. On the one hand the reader has obtained some decisive information about the character Steward. On the other, the elements of his reverie are central to the overarching themes the novel seems to consider: myths of foundation, the logic of social control, and the freedom-inspired drive toward a utopia, the "Paradise" of the book's title. Reading the passage in the context of these grand themes in turn allows a comparison of it with other historical discourses, which some scholars have done, for example the Americanist Katrine Dalsgard, who in a 2001 article relates it to the discourse of American exceptionalism. Dalsgard discusses how *Paradise* bears comparison to this recurrent movement in American literature and culture generally, based on the Puritan attempt at the founding of a New Jerusalem, the generational conflict produced by the disappointment in the failure in this dream, and the logic of subsequent violence employed on a scapegoat in an attempt to restore social order, famously represented, for example, in works like Nathaniel Hawthorne's *Scarlet Letter*.

Dalsgard's arguments are convincing and relevant to the intertextual, literary-historical positioning of Morrison's work. But not once does she actually relate the scene to the remembrance of the character Steward. My reading of the scene would focus on the importance of the "rememory" to Steward himself. The passage reveals the types of memories this character has, in whom more than any other the logic of the social order is symbolized, and who will design the attack on the Convent and murder its matriarch Consolata. While the passage thus associates the myths of Ruby's foundation with the patriarch of the text, it also in fact humanizes him by showing him capable of love and weakness. The passage would not be complete if we did not in fact read the truly tender lines which end it: "Sleep without the fragrance of her hair next to him was impossible" (100). There are always many undecideables in Morrison and her characters are always morally multifaceted. The very moral complexity of the characters is in fact a challenge: how do we make sense of a murderer who truly does love his wife? I don't think the text simply wants us to condemn Steward, but it does figure the inversion of the authority for which he stands.

Steward and his twin brother Deek together are a figure for a phallogocentric regime of signification; they are characters but also ciphers for the maintenance of a hierarchical social order, whose logic inevitably leads to violent exclusion of the marginalized, in an American exceptionalist discourse or otherwise. This same logic undermines the order itself with equal inevitability. In the culmination of the novel, the twins with seven other men go to the Convent with the intention to kill the odd group of women living there, including Consolata, their matriarch and spiritual leader, who also happens to be Deek's former adulterous lover of twenty years past. When Steward raises his gun to shoot Consolata, Deek unsuccessfully tries to prevent him. This leads to the first-ever rift between the twins, a symbolic split within the unity of phallic authority. The splitting of the twins parallels symbolically what Morrison, with grave graphicness, describes as the third eye ("the third one, wet and lidless" 291) staring from the bullet wound in Consolata's forehead, and these two figures form the difference inserted into the binary hierarchical textual and social structures and resist the closure after which they seek. The third eye becomes the brutally ironic inversion of the furrow in the brow from the Oven inscription, and marks the symbolic victory in defeat of matriarchal over patriarchal values, a permanent witness to the self-defeating ruse of hierarchal reason. In this culminatory scene, it is Deek's forgotten but unextinguishable love for Consolata that undoes the logic of the social order that led to Steward's hatred and ability to murder. Attention to the interaction of narrative time and characterization thus can point to the figural movement in the novel's textual dynamics which positions the redemptive power of love over the repressive violence of a hierarchical order.

Works Cited

Dalsgard, Christine. "The One All-Black Town Worth The Pain: (African) American Exceptionalism, Historical Narration, and the Critique of Nationhood in Toni Morrison's *Paradise*." *African American Review,* Vol. 35.2 (2001): 233-248.

Morrison, Toni. *Beloved*. New York: Plume, 1987.

—. *Jazz*. New York: Plume, 1993.

—. *Paradise*. New York: Plume, 1997

Rose, Charlie. Interview with Toni Morrison. 20 Jan. 1998.

Walker, Margaret. *Jubilee*. New York: Bantam, 1966.

Williams, Sherley Anne. *Dessa Rose*. New York: Harper Collins, 1999.

TRUTH VERSUS KNOWLEDGE: LAPLANCHEAN AFTERWARDSNESS AND THE TRAUMATIC MEMORY OF CHAPPAQUIDDICK IN JOYCE CAROL OATES' *BLACK WATER*

MATTHEW O. CLEVELAND

> It must be recognized as a memory, a distorted one, it is true, but nevertheless a memory. It has an obsessive quality; it simply must be believed. As far as its distortion goes it may be called a delusion; in so far as it brings to light something from the past it must be called truth.
>
> Sigmund Freud, *Moses and Monotheism* 205

In this short passage from *Moses and Monotheism*, Sigmund Freud proposes that the rise of Monotheistic religion is in part a function of the return of a 'truth' in the guise of delusion. Freud refers to this 'truth' as an "historical truth" and differentiates it from "material truth" inasmuch as it conveys not verifiable certainties, but rather a clue about–or "trace" of–particular foundational structures of (collective) identity (204-5). For Freud, the vehicle of this truth is memory–a hitherto repressed memory of trauma that irresistibly returns. Freud's musings here are indicative not only of the complexity and centrality of memory within his extensive discourse, but also of the ambivalent character that the concept of truth holds for the psychoanalytic enterprise. Within Joyce Carol Oates' novella *Black Water*, in which a fictionalized account of Ted Kennedy's infamous incident at Chappaquiddick is presented, both the structural complexity of memory and the ambivalent character of truth are broached.

The notorious incident that Oates' novel engages occurred on July 19, 1969 at Chappaquiddick, Massachusetts, where Senator Edward Kennedy drove off a wooden bridge in an accident that led to the drowning death of his passenger, 28-year-old Mary Jo Kopechne. This incident is widely recognized to be one of the key factors that ended Kennedy's presidential prospects. Indeed, the specter of this event continued to haunt Kennedy's senatorial career well into the 1990s, emerging to compromise his influence and credibility at critical junctures such as during the Senate Judiciary Committee inquiry into the sexual harassment case brought against Clarence Thomas by Anita Hill,[1] as well as during the investigation concerning the rape case brought against Kennedy's nephew William Smith.[2] This profound and enduring pressure that the Chappaquiddick incident has exerted upon Kennedy's life has in large part been a function of public speculation surrounding the senator's culpability. The incident itself is certainly well known, but official accounts of it–including Kennedy's public statement–are lacking in detail and fraught with inconsistency.[3] In her novella, Oates provides a fictional account of the incident (and events leading up to it) via a unique narrative contemplation of these omissions and inconsistencies.

In structural terms, *Black Water* can be understood according to how its narrative bears out the contradictory/oscillating mechanisms of traumatic anamneses. Oates' narrative descriptions of the events leading up to the drowning, and the drowning itself, are primarily delivered in third person and interspersed by remembered fragments of dialogue, commentary on a range of topics, and the (first person) delusive imaginings experienced by the protagonist while drowning. These components are presented in a fragmentary and chronologically disjunctive way. And although the chief narrator assumes a seemingly impassive and objective tone, the effect of this impassivity against what is conveyed is one that is provocative because what is produced is a voyeuristic proximity to the unfolding drama and horror experienced by the protagonist. This is evident from the very onset of the narrative:

> The rented Toyota, driven with such impatient exuberance by The Senator, was speeding along the unpaved road, taking turns in the giddy skidding slides, and then with no warning, somehow the car had gone off the road and had overturned in black rushing water, listing to its passenger's side, rapidly sinking.
> *Am I going to die? – like this?* (3)

---

[1] During the time of the inquiry, various commentators raised concerns about Kennedy's integrity as one of the senior Democrats who reviewed the case against Thomas. For example, in an article featured in *Time* magazine, Barbara Ehrenreich asks, "… isn't this a little like asking Michael Milken to monitor the SEe [Securities and Exchange Commission]?"(104). See also Fred Bruning's article "Comeuppance for a Kennedy" featured in *Maclean's*.

[2] See for example an article featured in the May 1991 issue of *Maclean's* by Tom Fennell and William Lowther titled "A deepening sex scandal" as well as Elanor Clift's *Newsweek* piece "A Problem With Women."

[3] See Robert Sherrill's *The Last Kennedy* and *Chappaquiddick: The Real Story* by James E. T. Lange and Katherine Dewitt Jr.

This opening passage depicts one of the scenes that the narrative returns to again and again via the protagonist's own obsessive fixations whilst drowning. Even though we are familiar at–or before–the outset with the outcome of this drama, we are nevertheless compelled into a mixture of fascination and dread with the presentation of such an intimate expression of trauma.

In bridging disparate theorizations surrounding both Jean Laplanche's development of the Freudian concept of *Nachträglichkeit* (as 'afterwardsness') and Jacques Lacan's oppositional paradigm between Truth and Knowledge, the present study will analyze the relationship between trauma and memory as it is presented in *Black Water*. The aim of this analysis will be to identify the ethical coordinates of Oates' text in relation to current debates *apropos* the accountability of literary representations of traumatic or traumatizing historical events.

Understanding *Black Water* as an Account of *Nachträglichkeit*

Freud, as part of his later-abandoned 'Theory of Seduction,' initially developed the term *Nachträglichkeit* in order to posit a relationship between memory and trauma whereby the (repressed) trauma pertaining to a discrete event is retroactively triggered by a later ostensibly unrelated event.[4] With Jean-Bertrand Pontalis in *The Language of Psycho-Analysis*, Laplanche initially outlines *Nachträglichkeit* as a process in which:

> ... the subject revises past events at a later date (*nachträglich*), and that it is the revision which invests them with significance and even with efficacity of pathogenic force. (112)

In other words, *Nachträglichkeit* describes a process by which the experience of trauma is initially not registered because the subject lacks the understanding to place that trauma in a context that is meaningful (i.e. traumatic). This trauma, which remains latent until it emerges in connection with a seemingly unrelated

---

[4] The theoretical utility of *Nachträglichkeit* has been explored in various capacities by a number of theorists. Some of the more notable thinkers who have engaged with *Nachträglichkeit* include Jacques Lacan ("The Function and Field of Speech and Language in Psychoanalysis" in *Écrits*), Jacques Derrida ("Freud and the Scene of Writing" in *Writing and Difference*), and Jean-François Lyotard (in various publications). It is, however, Jean Laplanche's development of *Nachträglichkeit* as 'afterwardsness' (*après-coup*) that will be employed in the present study because we believe that it offers the most expedient means of delineating the complex links between trauma, memory, and ethics in Oates' text.

occurrence, is only experienced as trauma *after* the subject acquires the knowledge necessary to grasp the originary experience as one that is traumatic. However, even at this point, the subject is not able to consciously link this trauma to the originary event.

In order to apply the concept of *Nachträglichkeit* to the representational nexus between trauma and memory in *Black Water*, at least two related contingencies require consideration. In the first place, even though it is almost painfully drawn out through the entire narrative, the protagonist's experience of drowning is shortly followed by her death. Indeed, in 'real time,' only moments transpire between what occurs on the above-quoted first page of the novella, where the protagonist–as the Senator's car is overwhelmed by "black rushing water"–asks, "*Am I going to die?– like this?*" (3), and the last page, in which the same "black water" is described to finally "fill her lungs" (154). What this means is that if the notion of *Nachträglichkeit* is to be applied to the representation of the relationship between memory and trauma in *Black Water*, the experience of drowning–despite its structural centrality to the plot–cannot be conceived as the originary traumatic event. Rather, it is necessary to understand the drowning event as the *trigger* for the meaningfulness of a prior and hitherto latent trauma to emerge, one that only acquires traumatic significance in the context of the protagonist's drowning.

So that if it is indeed the case that the protagonist's drowning serves only as a trigger, a second issue with discovering commensurability between the notion of *Nachträglichkeit* and Oates' narrative arises in that the identity of the originary trauma is not explicit for the protagonist. No 'moment of truth' materializes for the protagonist whereby she *consciously* connects her experience of trauma with a specific moment or entity. And that the experience of drowning for the protagonist is not itself yet registered as traumatic is demonstrated not least by the tone of incredulity that accompanies her conscious recognition of her impending demise as her own lungs fill with malevolent black water. This is comparable with Freud's case study of Emma, in which a girl of 8 is sexually molested by a shopkeeper but fails to register the trauma of the event. In his analysis, Freud discovers a link between this episode and an account the subject provides of a subsequent and seemingly extraneous incident in which she is an adolescent and experiences anxiety and distress when, in a different store altogether, she witnesses the banal scene of two store clerks sharing a laugh. As is the case for the protagonist in *Black Water*, the subject of Freud's study does not herself recognize the link between the originary event and the trauma she experiences during the subsequent event. In *Life and Death in Psychoanalysis*, Laplanche examines Freud's case study and explains that:

> Neither of the two events in itself is traumatic ... The first one? It triggers nothing: neither excitation or reaction, nor symbolization or psychical

elaboration; we saw why: the child, at the time she is the object of an adult assault, would not yet possess the ideas necessary to comprehend it. ... If the first event is not traumatic, the second is, if possible, even less so. (41-42)

Mutatis mutandis, in *Black Water*, we are presented with a range of disjointed scenes and observations with a certain dispassionate objectivity. Although both the narrator's remarks and the thoughts of the drowning protagonist that are presented are not entirely without affect, differentiation between the commonplace musings about astrological 'star signs' or romance and the more pointed considerations about politics and ideology is difficult. This, of course, is a function of the lack of any sense of topical or temporal ordering for these scenes and observations. These fragments are, moreover, interspersed with both the delusive imaginings of the protagonist about being rescued by the Senator, and 'real-time' snatches delineating the physical horror of the car accident and drowning. This topical and temporal entanglement is evident, for example, in the following passage:

> She'd never loved any man, she was a good girl but she would love that man if that would save her.
> The black water was splashing into her mouth, there was no avoiding it, filling her lungs, and her heart was beating in quick erratic lurches laboring to supply oxygen to her fainting brain where she saw so vividly jagged needles rising like stalagmites—what did it mean? Laughing ruefully to think how many kisses she'd had tasting of beer? Wine? Whiskey? Cigarettes? Marijuana?
> You love the life you've lived, there is no other.
> You love the life you've lived, you're an American girl. You believe you have chosen it.
>
> And yet: he *was* diving into the black water, diving to the car, his fingers outspread on the cracked windshield and his hair lifting in tendrils, *Kelly*? – *Kelly*? (152)

Here, descriptions of the material experience of "black water" invading her lungs are juxtaposed at once against the protagonist's fantasy of being rescued by the Senator and conferring him with her love, as well as her rueful consideration of the hollowness of 'American dream' platitudes and the intoxicated kisses of strangers.

Despite the disorder with which components of the narrative are arranged, it is nevertheless possible for us, as witnesses to this drama, to deduce that it is in fact the Senator, or at least the protagonist's encounter with him, that is the cause of the originary trauma. This is primarily because we bring to our encounter of the text the knowledge that the narrative enacts a speculative exploration of what has been omitted from official accounts of the Kennedy-

Chappaquiddick incident. With this foreknowledge, it becomes clear how the unnamed Senator is the most recurrent feature of the narrative and that he is in some way linked, by both the narrator and the protagonist, to each image and observation of the confused flotsam. In other words, the Senator functions as what Jacques Lacan calls the *sinthome* for the narrative.[5] The haunting specter of his presence serves to suture every other aspect of an otherwise chaotic array. To more clearly apprehend the significance of this structural disposition of the unnamed Senator, it is necessary to consider it in relation to the way in which Laplanche develops Freud's notion *of Nachträglichkeit.*

Laplanchean Afterwardsness and the Desire of the Other

What distinguishes Laplanche's notion of 'afterwardsness' from Freudian *Nachträglichkeit* is its emphasis upon a third term in the dialectic between remembering and (mis)identification. According to Laplanche, Freud only takes into account the relation or psychical trajectory between the subject before s/he encounters an originary trauma and the same subject after that trauma is triggered by a secondary event. What is missing in this equation is a third factor that, in effect, operates as the actual catalyst for the subject's reinterpretation of the originary trauma as trauma.[6] This third factor that Laplanche identifies takes the form of the desire of the other. This alien desire is perceived by the subject not only as an invasive, foreign, and external force, but one that poses an indecipherable question. As Laplanche explains in an interview with Cathy Caruth:

> The reality of the other ... is absolutely bound to his strangeness. How does the human being [subsequently traumatized subject] ... encounter this strangeness? It is in the fact that the messages he receives are enigmatic. His messages are enigmatic because those messages are strange to themselves. (Caruth 27)

In a qualification that will become meaningful presently, Laplanche goes on to clarify that this otherness takes the form of the concrete other as opposed to the

---

[5] In *An Introductory Dictionary of Lacanian Psychoanalysis*, Dylan Evans notes that although the *sinthome* was developed by Lacan from his work on the symptom, it came to designate (in Lacan's later work) "a signifying formulation beyond analysis, a kernel of enjoyment immune to the efficacy of the symbolic" (189). In other words, unlike the symptom, the *sinthome* is not a 'trace' of *jouissance* but rather that which structures its Drive.

[6] The distinction between afterwardsness and *Nachträglichkeit* is elucidated in greater detail in numerous texts including Paul Sutton's essay "Afterwardsness in Film."

Lacanian big Other (viz., the Symbolic Order that mediates social reality).
Notwithstanding this qualification, what Laplanche's words indicate for our
present reading is that the key to understanding the trauma of the protagonist
lies in pinpointing the effect of the alien strangeness (incarnated by the other)
upon her. In the following scene, which the protagonist remembers shortly prior
to her demise, this alien strangeness is borne out as the insatiable and
penetrating desire of the Senator:

> As he kissed her those several times, kissing, sucking groping as if, though they
> were standing fully clothed on a beach that, though not very populated, was
> nonetheless not deserted, he was in an agony to find a way into her, she felt a jolt
> of desire: not her desire, but the man's. As, since girlhood, kissing and being
> kissed, Kelly Kelleher had always felt, not her own, but the other's, the male's
> desire. Quick and galvanizing as an electric shock.
>   Feeling too, once she caught her breath, that familiar wave of anxiety, guilt –
> *I've made you want me, now I can't refuse you.* (115, emphasis in original)

It is axiomatic that the key component of this scene is the ambivalence that is
experienced by the protagonist: she encounters at once pleasure at being the
object-cause (*objet petit à*) of the alien masculine desire, and guilt about her
putative role in engendering the desire of the violating other. This ambivalence
is properly hysterical since in psychoanalysis the nosological designation of
hysteria is characterized by questions such as, 'What am I to the Other?', 'What
does the Other want from me?', and so on.[7] In his own application of
Laplanche's afterwardsness effect to the treatment of trauma in Alfred
Hitchcock's *Spellbound*, Richard Rushton speculates of Freud's Emma case
study:

> … it is not the nature of the hidden memory that is important in trauma: Emma's
> phobia does not arise as a result of her having been sexually violated by the
> shopkeeper and the subsequent repression of this violation. The essence of her
> trauma is not reducible to her repression of the shopkeeper's actions; his
> grabbing cannot in any way be said to have *caused* the trauma. […] … rather
> than being the *event* of the shopkeeper's actions that is crucial to the trauma, it is
> the *pleasure* obtained from the grabbing that is repressed by Emma, a pleasure
> that is repressed "afterwards," after Emma's introduction to a fully sexual world,
> and which introduces the trauma retroactively. (374, emphasis in original)

Rushton's theorization about the *true* origin of Emma's trauma presents us with
a fitting heuristic through which to elucidate the guilt and anxiety that the
protagonist of *Black Water* experiences in her encounter with the Senator's

---

[7] See Slavoj Žižek's *The Ticklish Subject* (249).

desire. In this vein, it is possible to argue that what is repressed by the protagonist is in fact the ambivalent pleasure/guilt that she experiences in response to the Senator's othered desire. This pleasure-guilt is, in the final instance, the uncanny *truth* that engenders the acephalous sense of trauma staining the fragments and snatches that comprise the narrative. The ambivalent nature of this truth raises certain questions with regards to the commensurability between our present theoretical framework and the contemporary debate surrounding the ethical status of literary narratives that depict the past.

The Ethics of Truth *contra* Knowledge

In his essay "Mending the Skin of Memory: Ethics and history in contemporary narratives" Tim Woods contemplates the healing capacity of literature that engages with historically traumatic events. Vis-à-vis the putative ethics of postmodern 'micro-narratives' and postcolonial 'counter-histories,' Woods posits:

> Conceiving of history as a national or racial trauma which needs to be healed or cured, is frequently offered as a reason for the retrieval of the past. Literature is one mechanism for effecting this ethical relation with the past. It provides a medium in which to imaginatively retrace the past and, in exhuming the forgotten events, offers a means of overcoming any instability, insecurity or reification of the past. (347)

Woods' reference to "the ethical relation with the past" is one that draws from both the Emmanuel Levinas gesture of an openness towards the other (341), as well as the Kristevan 'ethical imperative' which seeks to destabilize conceptions of identity, meaning, and truth (342-3).[8] Needless to say, although *Black Water* can indeed be considered a postmodern 'micro-narrative,' Woods' notion of ethics is not one that is fully amenable to the present psychoanalytic account. *Black Water* certainly presents a version of a historically traumatic event that calls into question the verity of established and hegemonic accounts of it. Nevertheless, as we have demonstrated, not only is the other (and *his* desire) in Oates' novella one who is characterized as a menacing force, but the narrative's structurally circular recreation of the protagonist's trauma resists any sense of resolution or hope.[9] Moreover, in contrast to the Kristevan ethical stance of

---

[8] See also Woods' collaborative effort with Peter Middleton, *Literatures of Memory*. This text provides descriptions of a wide range of authors and theoretical frameworks germane to the debate on the ethical implications of representing the past.

[9] Since the beginning of the narrative coincides with its conclusion, a nightmarish effect is produced in which the protagonist is perpetually experiencing the throes of a drowning

rejecting moral messages,[10] Oates' dystopic vision is clearly founded upon a didactic standard of morality that is unquestionably subjective. In his own (Lacanian) (re)deployment of afterwardsness, Rushton argues that the recognition of the source of a trauma does not necessarily lead to healing:

> For psychoanalysis, it is not merely the representational remembering of an original trauma that is at stake; it is not the unearthing of an ultimate event at the heart of the subject's symptoms that can guarantee a cure. Rather, the representative remembering of an originary trauma is but one step—and perhaps a minor one at that—along the path of psychoanalytic treatment. (372)

Therefore, from a psychoanalytic standpoint, if we agree with Rushton that trauma is not resolvable via the identification of its source, what ethical value *does* Oates' narrative carry?

Within Lacanian psychoanalysis, the notion of 'truth' always pertains to truth about desire (which is always subjective and subjectivating), whereas Knowledge refers to 'knowledge in the real'–a kind of acephalous non-subjectivized knowledge. In *The Plague of Fantasies*, Slavoj Žižek explains this Lacanian opposition between truth and knowledge as the difference between interpretation and construction. He notes of the analyst-analysand relationship:

> an interpretation is a gesture which ... aims to bring about the effect of truth apropos of a particular formation of the unconscious (a dream, a symptom, a slip of the tongue ...): the subject is supposed to 'recognize' himself in the signification proposed by the interpreter, precisely in order to subjectivize this signification, to assume it as his own ... The very success of interpretation is measured by this 'effect of truth', by the extent to which it *affects the subjective position of the analysand* (stirs up memories of hitherto deeply repressed traumatic encounters, provokes violent resistance ...). In clear contrast to interpretation, a construction (typically: that of a fundamental fantasy) has the status of a knowledge which can never be subjectivized–that is, it can never be assumed by the subject as the truth about himself, the truth in which he recognizes the innermost kernel of his being. (35-36)

As a heuristical device, this opposition between Truth and Knowledge offers a substantive means through which an ethical comparison between *Black Water* and official accounts of the Chappaquiddick incident can be conducted. In the first place, it is clear that the latter serves the function of non-subjectivized knowledge. In presenting an authoritative and hegemonic version of an incident that has had a far-reaching political and social impact, these accounts serve not only to desubjectivize the drowning victim of Kennedy's folly, but also to

---

death.
[10] See Middleton and Woods pp. 74-78.

negate the collective (intersubjective) investment in the ideological and idealistic rhetoric of the American Democratic party. And it is precisely this operation that gave rise to such a sense of betrayal amongst Kennedy's hitherto faithful electorate. As indicated above, Laplanche conceives of the other in his formulation as the 'small' concrete other person. However, within the context provided by Oates' novella, it is also possible to consider the Senator as a metonym for the Lacanian big Other that has somehow betrayed and thus hystericized not only the protagonist and the narrator, but the reader as well. It is certainly notable that not only does the Senator remain nameless, but for the protagonist, his identity is itself not enduring.

In contrast to the 'knowledge' offered by official accounts of the Chappaquiddick incident, Oates' narrative serves the purpose of construction. Its effect upon us (as readers/witnesses) is–to use Žižek's phrase–a 'truth effect' in that it allows us to recognize in its phantasmatic construction a materialization of the truth about our own desires, suspicions, and therefore origins. It is in this way that via her text, Oates gestures towards a radical ethics of delineating the past: more than simply providing a counter-narrative to a historically traumatic event, *Black Water* tethers itself to a subjectivized truth that renders the master-narrative–or the Master's narrative–superfluous.

Works Cited

Bruning, Fred. "Comeuppance for a Kennedy." *Maclean's*. 104.45 (1991): 15.

Caruth, Cathy. "An Interview With Jean Laplanche." *Postmodern Culture*. 11.2 (2001) <http://80-muse.jhu.edu.libproxy.stcloudstate.edu/journals/ postmodern_ culture/v011/11.2caruth.html>

Clift, Eleanor. "A Problem With Women." *Newsweek*. 117.22 (1991): 19-23.

Derrida, Jacques. *Writing and Difference*. Chicago: U. Chicago P., 1978.

Ehrenreich, Barbara. "Women Would Have Known." *Time*. 138.16 (1991): 104.

Evans, Dylan. *An Introductory Dictionary of Lacanian Psychoanalysis*. London: Routledge, 1997.

Fennell, Tom, and William Lowther. "A deepening sex scandal." *Maclean's*. 104.21 (1991): 28-29.

Freud, Sigmund. *Moses and Monotheism*. Trans. Katherine Jones. Letchworth, Hertfordshire: Hogarth, 1939.

Lacan, Jacques. *Écrits: A Selection*. Trans. Bruce Fink. New York: Norton, 2004.

Lange, James, and Katherine Dewitt Jr. *Chappaquiddick: The Real Story*. New York: St. Martins Press, 1993.

Laplanche, Jean. *Life and Death in Psychoanalysis*. Trans. Jeffery Mehlman. Baltimore: John Hopkins U.P., 1985.

Laplanche, Jean, and Jean-Bertrand Pontalis. *The Language of Psycho-Analysis*. Trans. Donald Nicholson-Smith. New York: Norton, 1973.

Middleton, Peter, and Tim Woods. *Literatures of Memory: History Time and Space in Postwar Writing*. Manchester: St. Martin's Press, 2000.

Oates, Joyce Carol. *Black Water*. New York: Dutton, 1992.

Rushton, Richard. "The Psychoanalytic Structure of Trauma: Spellbound." *Journal for Cultural Research*. 8.3 (2004): 371-384.

Sherrill, Robert. *The Last Kennedy*. New York: Dial, 1976

Sutton, Paul. "Afterwardsness in Film." *Journal for Cultural Research*. 8.3 (2004): 385-405.

Woods, Tim. "Mending the Skin of Memory: Ethics and history in contemporary narratives." *Rethinking History*. 2.3 (1998): 339-348.

Žižek. Slavoj. *The Plague of Fantasies*. London: Verso, 1997.

—. *The Ticklish Subject: The Absent Centre of Political Ontology*. London: Verso, 1999.

Part II

(Re)constructing the Caribbean: Memory and History

MASKS, MIRRORS, MIRTH AND MEMORY IN RANE ARROYO'S *HUNGRY GHOST: THE PONCE DE LEÓN POEMS*

ROBERT MILTNER

Chicago-born poet Rane Arroyo explores history and heritage in his poetic sequence *Hungry Ghost: The Ponce de León Poems*, originally published in *The Caribbean Writer*, then included as a section of Arroyo's 2002 collection *Home Movies of Narcissus*. In this poetic sequence, Arroyo, as person, poet, and *Puertorriqueño*, engages in a dialogue with the notorious historical figure of Ponce de León. He discovers first, he is both as present in history as history is present in him, second, while he "plumbs the depths of self …[he] comes up … altered by each freshly voiced exploration" (Leslie 316), and third, he uses masks, mirrors, mirth, and memory to complete the dialogue.

Hungry Ghost offers a continuation of Arroyo's "ongoing attempt to invoke and speak with figures from a cultural and personal past" (Sandlin 3). In order to transgress the boundaries of time and place which separate Arroyo from de León, readers observe Arroyo travel through time via poetry, in much the same way poet Tess Gallagher discusses this act in her essay "The Poem as Time Machine":

> The poem as a time machine works in an opposite way from the time machine as used in H. G. Wells. In the latter, one is sent out like a lonely projectile into time past or future, casting the present into a future or a past. The poem, on the other hand, is like a magnet which draws into it events and beings from … possible past, present, and future contexts of the speaker. (95-6)

When de León returns to the present time to seek out Arroyo, he discovers that though "History was easy once," things upon his return are more *complicated* than when he left:

> … my old islands
> now have skyscrapers instead of palm trees.
>
> My poor hysterical Hispañola is

  unhusbanded without me; Puerto Rico
      turns *pobre*. (40)

The poem is the magnet that draws Arroyo and de León together, and history is the room in which they meet. When the poem transports de León from the Puerto Rican historical past into Arroyo's own Ohio present, Arroyo must additionally bring his personal past as a poet into the present as, in a self-reflexive move, he dons the mask of the public poet in which he is ironically the mirrored image of his own poetic self. In "The Poet Rejects Ponce de León's Offer to Be a Muse," Arroyo ultimately accepts the offer:

  Well, one poem then,
  a catered exorcism,
  a bon voyage for bones (42)

Afterward, in "The Poet Shakes Off Ponce de León's Hungry Ghost," he will confess "The ventriloquist's séance/ last night was a bust" (48). Perhaps this arrangement is doomed from the start from inappropriate motive.

  Because de León fears historical anonymity, he seeks "Someone to help me flee forever the footnote" (40). He dispatches his ghost to ask Arroyo to write an epic for him—actually, *about* him—since it is art, not history, which grants immortality and eternal youth. The initial irony is immediately evident: here is de León, known in the popular culture as the historical figure who foolishly pursued the illusory *Fountain of Youth*, now foolishly pursuing Arroyo, demanding he write an illusory Epic de León, as it might be called, in order to be granted (apparently from the afterlife) immortality and eternal youth. What de León seeks is what the Franco-Czech writer Milan Kundera, in his novel *Immortality*, labels *Great Immortality*, that is, "the memory of a person in the minds of people who never knew him personally" (51). De León's ironic request, however, relegates him to the position of what Kundera labels *Ridiculous Immortality*; he offers the example of former US President Jimmy Carter who had a mild heart attack while jogging with reporters so that "instead of an athlete bursting with health [the cameramen] had to show an ageing man with bad luck" (52). As a result of *Ridiculous Immortality* therefore, one is remembered not as the hero of the moment but as its failure, the goat, the zero. Regardless of our self-projections, Kundera seems to suggest, we are judged and remembered by others based on their perceptions. How ironic, then, that a young Ponce de León boasts "I am my own meaning" (46), for history ascribes meaning, not individuals. The historic de León, the first of the Spanish explorers to visit and name Florida, was named Puerto Rico's first Governor; shortly after, he

...forced the [native] Taínos to work in the mines and to construct fortifications. The Tainos subsequently died in great numbers after exposure to the European diseases the sailors brought with them and to which the natives were not yet immune. ("Juan Ponce de León")

Through his participation in the destruction of the native culture at the hands of colonization, de León wasted his opportunity for true heroic action as humanitarian protagonist in lieu of his participation in oppression, relegating himself instead to the role of humanitarian antagonist. What must have seemed to de León the great deed of the moment—gold and glory—is remembered sadly:

> We all speak sorrow, son.
> It's the language of history. (49)

De León, who wants praise, not sorrow, has already traded his ticket for historical immortality at the wrong counter, and will get the Epic of the Buffoon, instead of the Epic de León.

While that 'serious character' of Modernism, Ezra Pound, supposedly dismissed the epic as merely a poem with history in it, an epic is defined as "a long narrative poem, typically a recounting of history or legend or of the deeds of a national hero" (Frye et al. 170), and it has at its center "a heroic or quasi-divine figure on whose actions depend[s] the fate of a tribe, a nation, or the human race" (Abrams 51). Ponce de León is part of the colonization of the New World with its "cruel policy initiated by Columbus and pursued by his successors [which] resulted in complete genocide" (Zinn 7) of the native populations of the Caribbean; the priest chronicler Bartolomé de las Casas, for example, estimated that between 1494 and 1508, "over three million people had perished from war, slavery, and the mines" (Zinn 7) in Hispañola alone. Certainly, then, de León, who was a part of that colonization and genocide, was, in his way, "a quasi-divine figure"–which may be why Arroyo will not write de León a "*winged* epic" (my italics), and certainly his actions, like other colonizers, made "the fate of the tribe" dependent on his actions. Moreover, though some Renaissance critics ranked the epic as "the highest of all *genres*" the epic was ranked by Aristotle himself as "second only to tragedy" (Abrams 51); given the tragedy of colonization and genocide in the Caribbean, an epic for de León would be second to tragedy of destruction on such a scale. Yet de León is willing to compromise on the nature of epic as long as there is one; he offers not be jealous of El Cid, as one of the poem's titles states, but encourages Arroyo to

> Learn that fever is both

the message and the messenger.
Write me a defense that distracts from facts.
The fountain between my legs, *poeta*,
that was history, the future, *el futuro*. (47)

Functioning as one of the "liminal presences that refuse to be laid to rest" (Sandlin 1), de León further warns Arroyo to

Learn, *hijito*—the accent mark
over the hard word "León" is
a savage knife falling from Heaven. (44)

Arroyo wisely takes de León seriously to some extent—one should always be cautious of hungry lions—for he hears de León muse how "This poet [Arroyo] has a piñata for a heart" (44) and that it is the function of poetry to "raise scars" (52).

Arroyo, although knowing "the age of epic is over," replies with a literary exorcism of several poems. Given Puerto Rico's colonial past, Arroyo expresses Lyotard's sense of "incredulity" towards Grand Narratives (xiv), and seeks what might be seen as minor narratives—anything short of the classical epic. The formal design for this is a sequence of poems which operates as a kind of anthology–using mock-epic, lyric, faux valediction, drama–gathered together into a "garland of poems," the term *anthology* coming from the Greek for garland, a bouquet of flowers ("Anthology"). This shift from epic to anthology, necessary for exploring the differences between de León and Arroyo, between past and present, offers an example of what Homi Bhabha sees as necessary for issues regarding postcolonial identity:

What is theoretically innovative, and politically crucial, is the need to think beyond narratives of originality and initial subjectivities and to focus on those moments or processes that are produced in the articulation of cultural differences. (764-765)

Seemingly, part of what constitutes cultural difference is the choice of genres, for genre expresses identity, either as the grand narrative of the egotistical epic or self-identity development of the lyric poem.

Some readers may notice that Arroyo's *Hungry Ghost* echoes the structure of Folgore Da San Gemignano's 13th-century *A Garland of Months* in its use of twelve poems which operate as a time-counting device, both for Folgore and Arroyo. Additionally, what Richard Aldington, Folgore's translator, says of 13th-century San Gemignano could equally be said of de León and his era:

> Then as now men might more truly and no less discouragingly be divided
> into Creators and Destroyers, those who make things and those who smash them.
> The vandals are always the vandals, whatever their excuses and motives. ("A
> Wreath for San Gemignano" 11)

Aldington and Folgore, de León and Arroyo: all move through time, or have
time move through them, as means of self-definition, both in their lifetimes and
after. What emerges from the bantered dialogue between Arroyo and de León,
then, is a series of considerations and meditations on the nature of youth,
literature, history, and culture, and these issues and others join Arroyo on the
stage as he picks up his mask.

Reginald Harris, in a review of *Home Movies of Narcissus*, observed that
many of Arroyo's poems deal with "acting, masks, and the taking on of
personas" (1). Having successfully donned masks in *The Singing Shark*, his
previous book, as he stepped into the personas of Juan Angel and The Singing
Shark (a member of the Puerto Rican gang from the musical *West Side Story*),
Arroyo extended this technique to a larger sequence in *Hungry Ghost*. In
"Promised Poem: Being Ponce de León," for example, Arroyo wears the mask
of de León so he can operate as a persona in the drama of history. Fittingly,
persona "was the Latin word for the mask used by actors in the classical theater,
from which was derived the term *dramatis personae* for the list of characters
who play a role in a drama" (Abrams 135). Inside this mask, Arroyo feels what
it is like to be the antagonist in the tragedy. Arroyo must choose to wear a mask
so that he can stand in the lyric center of de León, inside the lyric "I" from
which de León speaks; in doing so, Arroyo explores self-identity. Culture and
history connect Arroyo to de León, in the same way Arroyo connected with the
Puerto Rican father-figure, William Carlos Williams in "The Carlos Poems"
from *The Singing Shark*. When Arroyo addressed Williams by saying, "You are
one of us if only for the blood" (SS 62), he might as well have been addressing
de León, who reminds Arroyo that

> ... you have forgotten
> that Old Spain is your mother who
> demands blood. (*HMN* 52)

The poetic time machine, in this case, carries Arroyo into the past, into de León,
so that by standing in that lyric center he stands in the eye of what Ezra Pound
once called The Vortex, a swirling storm of culture, art, and history. This act
allows Arroyo to stand cloaked in culture, an actor standing body-forth on the
historical stage, a poet in the act of performance engaging the vortex of culture,
and appropriately so, for "Terms of cultural engagement, whether antagonistic
or affiliative, are produced performatively" (Bhabha 765). Further, de León's

statement that "My words, your mouth: an ancient trade route" (47) makes the *mask* a *mirror*. Now, the mask is a projection of our face-self out to the world; in the mirror, our face is the mask projected back.

In Kundera's *Immortality*, the central character Agnés obsesses over her constant encounters with human faces: we have to, she observes,

> ... get over our surprise that precisely this (what we see facing us in the mirror) is our self. Without the faith that our face expresses our self, without that basic illusion, that archillusion, we cannot live, or at least we cannot take ourselves seriously. (13).

Thus, for Arroyo/de León to take himself seriously—or to offer an ironic counterpoint—he must be both the mask and the lyric "I" or suffer a loss of credibility. In short, the reader is asked to imagine a ghost seeing itself in a mirror: Arroyo must haunt de León as de León haunts him.

Moreover, Arroyo haunts de León in a manner evoking Dorian Gray's face haunting him from the frame on the wall, the one face caught in an aging process while its mirror image remains a static product. Thus, by transgressing the boundaries of self by putting on the mask of an-other, Arroyo is empowered to overthrow de León, one of the "graying gods" (50). What is gained in this exchange is a reversal; what Arroyo seeks is to "be young forever" (50), to discover through poetic process rather than iconic product, and by "*masking*" himself, he succeeds, relegating de León to the role of icon where he remains static, limited like Dorian Gray, and replicable much like an endless wall of Andy Warhol silk screens, an iconographic product for the common market. De León, who sought immortality and epic status, becomes crystallized into an Apollonian father-figure, stern and gray. And Arroyo? Having "seen past the mirror" (UAP 1), he gets to play the role of Dionysius, the reveler and engenderer, the role that allows him to share the stage with Bacchus, Loki, Coyote, and other tricksters and transformers.

Empowered by this dynamism, Arroyo is able to be playful, witty, ironic: the whole toolbox of comedy (Aristotle's antithesis to tragedy, and therefore also ranked superior to the epic) provides for Arroyo to make mirth with the figure of de León. Poet Naton Leslie, in a review of *Home Movies of Narcissus*, praised the poems as "delightful, full of word play, even word collisions" (316-7). One example of this is found when Arroyo provides de León with an update on the state of things in Puerto Rico:

> We are wealthy with
> our plastic surgeons,
> plastic flatware,
> plastic flamingoes,
> plastic card calypsos. (41)

This list of puns—a sort of pun itself on the encyclopedic nature of epics—is so enjambed with puns that this quatrain nearly jumps the syntactic track. Arroyo "writes with humor and a remarkable quickness of associations ... with language that is ... mischievous" (UAP 1), as evident in the clever "Promised Poem, Second Attempt: A Young Ponce de León" which is a small drama of eight   voices, including Ponce, his father, his mother, a soldier, a nun, a neighbor, Christopher Columbus, and a chorus named "Voices."   When the young Ponce speaks about himself, he states:

> A sum summarizes as summons.
> The whole always hides holes (46)

Such quick associations demonstrate—through Arroyo's mask—both the young Ponce's mischievous nature as well as his numerical view of the world. The "Voices," which speak chorally four times, say only "Numbers. Numbers" (45-6), but who or what are these numbers? The forgotten famous conquerors, the innumerable conquered, the sheer volume of humanity that diminishes the acts of the individual, the sounds emitted by faces, or the ironic counterpoint to what the Nun identifies as the importance of the zero?   A Nun puns with the mathematical Zero which "we stole from The/ Sahara," confirming Spain's notion of empire and the theft which accompanies it, yet "Zero shares the egg's shape, eyeballs, balls" (45). The humor here is associative and clever: those who conquer get "the whole" Ponce referred to, while the conquered get zero, nothing. The egg is the world with its hemispheres, a world to be conquered by those who see and share that vision of empire with their "eyeballs." Yet the zero is also one without "balls," suggesting those who are conquered and emasculated from their own cultural construct of manhood, and also a zero is one who does not stand up for the rights of those being conquered. Ironically, a nun delivers this speech: of course, married to the church, she remains virgin, a zero of sorts, and she represents members of the religious who have at varied historical times both supported and resisted conquest and oppression: now you're zero, now you're not.

Finally, Arroyo discovers he must share in cultural memory to move beyond what de León calls the "terrible lie" (44) that is lyric poetry. After all, since lyrics are "brief and discontinuous, emphasizing sound and pictorial imagery rather than narrative or dramatic movement" (Frye et al. 268), they are too limited to engage in large scale cultural studies in anything less than a fragmented way; no wonder, then, that the lyric was long regarded as "a relatively minor form of poetry, better adapted to lesser poets than epic or drama" (Frye et al. 269-70). The de León mask allowed Arroyo to address the historical de León in a postmodern manner, using lyric fragmentation rather than epic chronology, brevity rather than scale, sound and image rather than catalogue, irony rather than exaggeration. Yet there are other underlying ironies here as well. Arroyo must modestly accept the limiting mantle of lesser or minor poet in order to craft a lyric, definitionally speaking, rather than assume major status as a writer of epics. Moreover, given de León's status as conquistador, as one whose arrival in the present demanding an epic celebration of his deeds, he represents the essence of historical *machismo*; on the other hand, given that Arroyo is a contemporary gay Latino poet, his selection by de León as his epic scribe is, by contrast, ironic. De León proves to be a realist, however, questioning whether he made the right choice for the task of elevating his historical status:

Isla, forgive our Arroyo for his conquering
words and not worlds; poets can be used to
to hide the bodies from historians and God. (53)

Ultimately though, his choice proves unsatisfactory to de León, the stern Apollonian, who dismisses Arroyo as a "clumsy ventriloquist" and an "amateur magician" (44). In the tenth poem in the sequence, his "War on Poets," de León recognizes his error of selection and seeks to correct it:

I will now haunt a historian, kinder
Fabulist. Arroyo, I kick you to the curb—
and take your hipped Ricky Martin with you. (52)

In essence then, de León fires Arroyo as his epic scribe, and "un-haunts" him, though Arroyo remains haunted in the aftermath of experiencing de León's ghost.

While de León dismissively states that poets are "memorialists with nothing to confess" (52), Arroyo learns nonetheless to confess the scars of history, of blood, and finally, of his need for "an honest ghost" to aid him, even if that ghost is de León: "I'll write these/ Ponce de León poems later, / when I'm old. Delirious …" (51) he writes in "The Exhausted Poet." The haunting of history is therefore necessary, for by connecting youth and age, past and present, history comes alive and the statues speak, as Arroyo discovers in the final poem in the sequence, "The Poet Dreams of a City Crowded with Singing Statues":

The young age in each
Other's dramas. …
………………………..
          The young
are replaced by the younger.
Where are my honest ghosts?

What is a son without a father?
Statues keep predicting the wrong past.
Ponce? de León? Juan? (55)

The ghost of the past is the father-figure for the poet son; history is not an isolated statue but a living presence in the present; and the present is familiar, alive, represented by Arroyo's shift from the formal "Ponce? de León?" to the familiar "Juan?"

As Betsy Sandlin notes, because Arroyo's writing is often "invested in self-[reflection] and metapoetic reflection," he is able to "invoke ghosts of the past in order to understand his own spectral present/presence" (1), which, in this case, is de León's ghost arriving in the present to haunt Arroyo. Yet the present, observes Homi Bhabha, "can no longer be simply envisaged as a break or a bonding with the past and the future, no longer a synchronic presence: our proximate self-presence, our public image, comes to be revealed for its discontinuities, its inequalities, its minorities" (767). For Rane Arroyo, it is history with its discontinuities, inequalities and miscommunications which haunts, and like a ghost, though it can be seen, does not answer. It can only question.

Works Cited

Abrams, M. H. *A Glossary of Literary Terms*, 5th ed. NY: Holt, Rinehart and Winston, 1988.

Aldington, Richard. *A Wreath for San Gemignano*. NY: Duell, Sloan & Pearce, 1945.

Arroyo, Rane. *Home Movies of Narcissus*. Tuscon, AZ: The University of Arizona Press, 2002.

—. *The Singing Shark*. Tempe, AZ: Bilingual Press, 1996.

Bhabha, Homi. "The Postcolonial and the Postmodern: The Question of Agency." *Criticism: Major Statements* 4th ed. Charles Kaplan and William Davis Anderson. Boston: Bedford/St. Martin's, 2000. 763-81.

Frye, Northrop, Sheridan Baker, and George Perkins. *The Harper Handbook to Literature*. NY: Harper & Row, 1985.

"Juan Ponce de León." Wikipedia. November 9, 2005. <http://en.wikipedia.org /wiki/Juan_Ponce_de_Leon>.

Kundera, Milan. *Immortality*. Trans. Peter Kussi. NY: Perennial, 1990.

Leslie, Naton. "Rev. of *Pale Ramón* by Rane Arroyo." *Ohioana Quarterly* (2000): 316-8.

Lyotard, Jean-François. *The Postmodern Condition: A Report on Knowledge.* Trans. Geoff Bennington and Brian Massumi. Minneapolis: U of Minnesota P, 1984, reprint 1997.

Sandlin, Betsy A. "Queer Hauntings: Metapoetic Ghosts in the Poetry of Rane Arroyo and Manuel Ramos Otero." Unpublished paper. Np Nd. University of Arizona Press. October 17, 2005. <http:// www.uapress.arizona.edu/CATALOGS/fall02>.

"Anthology." Wikipedia. October 25, 2005. <http://www.answers.com/topic /anthology.>

Wilde, Oscar. *The Picture of Dorian Gray.* London: Oxford University Press, 1974.

Zinn, Howard. *A People's History of the United States.* NY: Perennial, 2001.

RAÍCES ETERNAS: THE DOCUMENTARY FILM AS A PROJECT/ION OF PUERTO RICAN HISTORY

JOCELYN A. GÉLIGA VARGAS[1]

The intricate relationship that exists between history and the documentary film has been explored from three distinct but interconnected perspectives. The first approach subsumes the documentary to the project of narrating film history, or explicating the evolution of film as an artistic, industrial, aesthetic, technological and socio-cultural phenomenon. In this endeavor, the documentary is but one more genre factored into accounts about the development of cinema, often in reference to a particular geographic or national territory. Through this lens, documentary films are seen as "pieces of evidence" (Thompson and Bordwell 4) or documents whose "factual" status parallels that of the narrative film or the bibliographic source (Lagny 245).

Another way in which the relationship between the documentary film and history has been established is in the process of mapping out the evolution of the genre itself. The totalizing impetus of this enterprise propels art and film historians to search for the genesis of the form. Scholars who privilege the analysis of the documentary product set the origin of the genre in film history itself, namely in the *actualités* that resulted from the pioneer film experiments of the Lumière brothers. However, those historians who turn their attention to the documentary producer and the process of production conjure the legacy of preceding art and media forms. Film scholar and documentarist Michael Rabiger, for instance, argues that the true antecedents of the genre are in painting and caricature, two means of representation that paved the way for the documentary film of the twentieth century to depict actuality "from an individual and emotionally committed perspective" (10).

This recuperative search for a point of origin in documentary history is often paired with the drive to organize the corpus into self-contained categories that could be put to the service of an explanatory framework. Film theorist Bill Nichols, for instance, developed an influential documentary typology that

---

[1] The author wishes to thank Professors Alfredo González Martínez and Raymond Gómez for providing her with some of the research materials consulted in the process of writing this essay.

bespeaks a positivistic logic of causal chronology. In his article "The Voice of the Documentary," Nichols contends that generational redefinitions of the concept of realism have led to changing modes of expository discourse in the documentary genre. He locates the origin of the documentary tradition in John Grierson's *direct-address documentary*. This didactic model anchored its claims to realism in the presentation of "facts" about disregarded social experiences and, as Brian Winston has argued, "victimized" social subjects (269-272). The subsequent *cinéma vérité* style promised to increase the "reality effect" by capturing the actions of everyday life and eschewing the artifice of the "*voice of God*" commentary that characterized the Griersonian approach. The third documentary modality identified by Nichols is the *interview format*, in which the orchestration of the voices of witness-participants is believed to produce a less suspect rendition of reality than that rendered by the other two formats. It is a multiple-voiced realism in which neither the eye of the camera nor the single voice of the narrator commands the presentation of history. Finally, Nichols arrives at the more elusive *self-reflexive* documentary, in which the filmmaker reemerges as a participant and a fabricator of "reality" but lacks the authorial voice and rejects the privileged position of the Griersonian narrator.

In the third approach to the study of the documentary and history, the film ceases to be a piece of evidence that informs an exterior historical account and becomes itself becomes the historical account, the historical text, the narration of social history. Invoking the etymology of the term *documentary*–which is derived from the noun *document* (proof, evidence) and the verb document (to construct or produce with authentic situations or events)–film theorists like William Scott and Robert Coles shed light on this view of the documentary as history. For Scott, the genre straddles the realms of the public and the private: it furnishes decisive evidence about public events and social conditions, yet it is not objective but thoroughly personal (5-6). Hence, it is at once a socio-historical document and a human document that "carries and communicates feeling, the raw material of drama" (7). Coles evokes a similar tension but sketches it over the figure of the documentarist. In his view, the documentary filmmaker wages a twofold struggle (20). On one hand, the filmmaker attempts to ascertain what *is*, what can be noted, recorded, historically verified and substantiated. On the other, she/he must present what *is* in ways that can elicit the interest of others and recreate a context so that the incidents are connected to the conditions that prompted them. In this third approach, then, the documentary is indeed a record of history, a producer of what Nichols calls that "regard their relation to the real as direct, immediate, transparent" ("Representing" 3-4). Concomitantly, it is a testimony of the individual and emotional commitments invoked by Rabiger (10). Moreover, because the documentarist is herself a social and historical subject, I would contend that these commitments are always intertwined in a web of convictions and compromises that are collective, that reflect not just a personal but also a social positioning. In this sense, the documentary is not simply a projection of history but a project of historical fabrication articulated in the language of power and control that characterizes its epoch and context. In *The Writing of History* Michel de Certeau notes that when we study a historical text we do not come to know what actually happened in the past, but what has been reconstructed about the past (qtd. in Lagny 43). These reconstructions, he adds, are always shaped by implicitly or explicitly stated motives. If we grant the documentary the status of a historical text, we must then attend to its selective process of recreation of the past as well as to the underlying premises that guide it. This is the line of inquiry that I pursue in this work, considering the documentary *Raíces Eternas* as both a projection and project of Puerto Rican history. Before engaging in this analysis, however, I think it is pertinent to reconstruct the context in which the film was produced and distributed.

Raíces Eternas is an internationally prized documentary directed by Noel Quiñones and released in 1986, after seven years of epic exploits to marshal material and human resources for professional filmmaking in the context of a country that lacks both a film industry and stable incentives to promote this form of artistic production. At the time of its release, the film participated in film festivals in the US, garnered the Silver Award at the Houston International Film Festival, and was screened in several theatres across Puerto Rico. It has been repeatedly broadcast on Puerto Rican television during the past two decades and is often used as an educational resource for Puerto Rican History courses in local public schools.

Titled after a poem by Puerto Rican poet, journalist and politician José de Diego (1866-1918), the film could be read as a tribute to this figure and his nation-building deeds in the wake of the Spanish rule and the rise of the US colonial regime. Evoking this nationalistic spirit, director Noel Quiñones, in a 1986 interview, described his film as "an homage to our culture ... our most authentic contribution to the Hispanic-American world," which sets out to "cinematically register the historic and cultural trajectory of Puerto Rico, emphasizing the ethnic and civilizing roots of our development as a people" (qtd. in Borges 62). In the rhetoric of popular film critic Pedro Zervigón, *Raíces Eternas* is equivalent to "stepping into a time machine to traverse the history of Puerto Rico with the objective of exploring the diverse cultural influences that gave shape to the Puerto Rican character" (27). In his view, the forty-two minute film skillfully synthesizes the important events and fundamental aspects of the formation of Puerto Rican nationality through meticulous and faithful historical reconstruction.

Authorial intentions and critic impressions aside, we could describe the documentary as a reenactment of Puerto Rico's colonial history whose visuals are almost exclusively staged and meticulously produced representations of canonical historical events. This staging, however, is not *self-reflexive* in Nichols's terms: the film acknowledges neither its artifices nor the partiality of its truth. The filmmaker's (and his critics') claims to historical veracity and realism are anchored in the film's alleged loyalty to historical documents and the verisimilitude of its mise-en-scène. Moreover, to stabilize the polysemy of these deliberately crafted images, the film employs the Griersonian *voice of God* approach. The unrestricted and portentous voice-over narration, written after the visuals had been shot, directs the audience through the signifieds of the image, serving what Barthes calls an "anchorage function" (39-41). The linguistic message elucidates the iconic message but does so in a selective process that underscores only those signs that contribute to producing a progressive and ultimately harmonious narrative of cultural fusion and national conformation. A brief plot summary will illustrate this point and offer a context for my analysis, which regards the status of the documentary as both a projection and a project of (Puerto Rican) history by examining two specific sequences of the film.

Raíces Eternas opens with a series of title plates that establish the first setting of the story.[2] The year is 1492, the place is Spain, the plot is the Spanish thrust for imperialist expansion, the counterforce are *los musulmanes* (the Muslims). Above them rises the film's first and perhaps only individual protagonist, Cristóbal Colón, who, the plate indicates, challenges the conventional wisdom of his epoch and "in his first voyage discovers a vast continent that would change the course of history."[3] The following plate forwards us to 1493. Two sentences frame the reenactments that follow: "Cristóbal Colón embarks on his second voyage. This is the history of cultural roots, of triumphs and defeats, of might and hope that come together in the creation of a new race."[4]

The first diegetic visuals are a series of low-angle shots of the Spanish caravels as they face the treacherous waters and stormy skies of the Caribbean. The contrast in these shadowy and sinister nighttime shots is provided by a cream-colored mainsail, over which looms large the red and yellow-toned Royal

---

[2] The documentary's narration and title plates are entirely in Spanish. To facilitate the flow of my argument, I include only my English translations of the text in the body of this essay; when direct quotations are used I provide transcripts of the original Spanish passages in footnote references.

[3] *En su primer viaje, Colón habrá de descubrir un vasto continente que cambiará abruptamente el curso de la historia.*

[4] *Cristóbal Colón emprende su segundo viaje. Ésta es la historia de raíces culturales, de triunfos y derrotas, de fuerza y esperanza, que se unen en la creación de una nueva raza.*

Standard of the Catholic Kings.[5] Eerie music and wind sounds build up the disquieting effect of the sequence. But the tension is settled by the portentous *voice of God* that closes the sequence with the following assertion: "Threatened by storms and the uncertainty of being lost in a vast ocean, seventeen caravels and an army of men lusting for gold and glory open the doors to a new and fascinating adventure."[6]

The film then proceeds to string together nine chronological segments that reenact a series of historical events and myths. The first chapter is devoted to the "discovery" of Puerto Rico, the triumphant imperial penetration and exploration of *Boriquén*, which is symbolically represented in the figure of an *"india"* (Taína) who leads the Spanish army into the Island and offers them the sweet fluid they coveted: water.

The second segment treats the colonization period as a confrontation between civilization (Spanish Catholicism) and barbarism (Taíno myths and beliefs). Colonization, the narrator proclaims, foments the fusion of two races and plants the root of a new culture. Facing the loss of his land and his woman, the *"indio"* (Taíno) launches a *"suicidal attack"* against the Spanish; his predictable failure signals the futility of his beliefs and symbolizes the rise of the Spanish as the lords of the land. The vexed politics of cultural fusion are thus rhetorically concealed under the mantle of civilizing progress.

African drums mark the beginning of a short third segment that discursively justifies the "arrival" of the *negro africano* (black African) in Puerto Rico as a necessary measure for the economic success of the colony. The black race, the narrator anticipates, will become an important element in Puerto Rican society: it will evolve and be subsumed into a social body characterized by racial fusion. This integrationist discourse, however, is at odds with the iconic allegories of the sequence, which represent *negro* subjectivity in reference to two atavistic tropes. The first one is forced labor, signified by a lethargically moving line-up of enchained black males commanded by a white overseer, while the second trope is pain and injustice, symbolized by the branding of the black slave with the hot iron known as *el carimbo*.

The fourth segment is less a reenactment of canonical historical events than a mythological rendition of an arbitrarily partitioned historical period. Sepia tones help paint a rosy picture of 17th- and 18th-century Puerto Rico, an alleged period of national integration metonymically represented by the emerging coastal villas. In them the family—with the mother figure as a transmitter of

---

[5] A representation of the Royal Flag carried by Columbus on his expedition to the New World that stood as an emblem of the Spanish Crown from 1492 to 1506.

[6] *Acosados por tormentas y por la constante incertidumbre de estar perdidos ante un vasto océano, diecisiete carabelas y un ejército de hombres con sed de oro y gloria abren las puertas a una nueva y fascinante aventura.*

culture–and Christianity–with the Catholic Church as the symbol of culture–forge "the new Puerto Rican race," borne out of the combination of *indios*, *negros*, *blancos* and *mestizos*. Manual labor, we are told, is the thread that weaves them together and crafts the singularly splendid social fiber of Puerto Rican society.

In light of this conciliatory rhetoric, it is not surprising that the following segment sets out to erect a new counterforce against which our zealously patched national hero could rise. Back to historical events, the sequence recounts the 1797 British attack on Puerto Rico, during which civilians allegedly joined forces with the Spanish army to resist the "foreign" invasion. The closing shot frames the profile of a pensive *criollo* soldier,[7] slowly zooming out to reveal his upright body facing out of frame. The audio track alerts us that this is a simile: the virile body is the "*tronco firme*" (the unyielding trunk) that has sprouted from the ancient roots. Relentless before the invading enemy, adds the narrator, unity founds a new race, with a firm purpose and an authentic personality.

In this auspicious tone the documentary welcomes the 19th century, depicted as the crowning stage of the *nueva raza* (new race) in the context of new migrations, the abolition of slavery, and political and social reform. The aesthetically and expressively splendid shots evoke classic Hollywood iconography of the Great Migration or the Western Caravans. This time, however, it is the mountain *jíbaros* (*criollo* peasants) who solemnly march across the virginal landscape, crossing the frontier to the new millennium. In this threshold, proclaims the narrator, a "true Puerto Rican cultural, political and economic identity is manifested and affirmed" by heralds who reflect the diverse ethnic roots of our people.

The consecrated national hero, figured as the product of the absolute fusion of Taíno, Spanish and African "elements," faces another antagonist in the following segment. Adopting the colonial rhetoric, the segment casts the US as *el enemigo* (the enemy) that challenges the authority of the motherland, Spain. The American invasion of Puerto Rico is not visually recreated but is discursively acknowledged in these unequivocal terms. Its effects are anticipated and lodged exclusively in the realm of culture. As the segment's closing words connote, a new counterforce threatens the integrity of the national hero: "The American! a new cultural presence that asserts itself in the Island and that will

---

[7] From the sixteenth through the eighteenth century the term *criollo/a* was generally used in Puerto Rico to refer to white people born of Spanish parents in the colony. Thereafter people of European descent were often designated simply as *blancos* or *criollos blancos* to distinguish them from the *criollos negros*, who were the descendents of enslaved Africans born in Puerto Rico. This way *criollo* gradually came to mean born in Puerto Rico during the Spanish colonial regime (Wagenheim and Jiménez de Wagenheim 33).

exert significant influence on its future. Puerto Rico will continue to develop under this new tutelage, which is alien to its cultural roots."[8]

The last two segments are completely set in the 20th century. A brief one, and the only one containing archival material, is devoted to the natural catastrophes that beset the Western region of the Island in the 1910s. The closing segment, set in the 1980s, is a highly didactic and celebratory epilogue that wrestles to bring a sense of closure, taking recourse in the circular narrative. The film returns to the images and sounds of running water as the signifier of an "original encounter" between two currents that merged into one. Bridging that encounter and the "mutual process of discovery" between the Taíno and the Spanish, the Catholic Church reemerges as cultural unifier and spiritual guide of a unitary Puerto Rican history "in which we are all present." No prophetic words are uttered, but a welter of pronouncements intent on projecting the history of the nation as a jubilant feat of incorporation and assimilation. The Taíno race, we are told, has endured in Puerto Rican culture. The *"negro"* is no longer African but *puertorriqueño* because Puerto Rico has opened up and incorporated him. The American influence has been integrated by a people who do not forsake their heritage. The Puerto Rican diaspora is spread around the world but will eventually return home. And home, the narrator adds, is still the same paradise discovered by Columbus 500 years ago. The flimsily patched image of the contemporary *puertorriqueño* as the syncrisis of races begins to rip with this deference to colonial mythology and authority. But it is the closing title that pulls the stitches and unveils the underlying message of the film. It is a reproduction of the last stanza of the cited poem by José de Diego: "And even underneath the clear waves / Pound lively, headed east / The eternal Spanish roots."[9]

In light of this plot synopsis, we could summarily conclude that *Raíces Eternas* is indeed a historical document inasmuch as it grasps the historical realm. We could as well reason that, as a projection of history, the documentary is a selective, partial, and motivated reconstruction of historical events and processes. Because it is not, to use Nichols's terms, a *self-reflexive* documentary, its motives are positively subdued. Nonetheless, we could trace them down in the archives of official colonial history. The myth of the Puerto Rican melting pot (i.e., the equation of the Puerto Rican national to the sum of the Taíno, the Spanish, and the African) is a pillar of Puerto Rican historiography which strives to overshadow the multiple axes of power that rive the nation. Yet,

---

[8] *Una nueva cultura se hace sentir en la isla para ejercer importante influencia en su futuro: ¡el americano! Puerto Rico continuará su desarrollo bajo una nueva tutela, una que es extraña a sus raíces culturales.*
[9] *¡Y aún, por debajo de las claras olas, vivas palpitan, caminando a Oriente, las eternas raíces españolas!*

beside this additive and assimilationist trope rides the obstinate quest for an original root. The documentary jubilantly finds it in the figure of the Spanish. Fanon's words seem relevant and regrettably current: "Every colonized people . . . finds itself face to face with the language of the civilizing nation; that is with the culture of the mother country. The colonized is elevated above his jungle status in proportion to his adoption of the mother country's cultural standards" (18).

In *Raíces Eternas* the language of the "civilizing nation" seeps through in multivocal ways. I have demonstrated that the narrative echoes the official history of Puerto Rican colonization, enshrining the Hispanic essence of our alleged collective character. On the other hand, and at a less apparent level, the historical project that the documentary undertakes follows the tracks of colonialist film history. As Robert Stam has persuasively argued, the beginnings of cinema coincided with the height of imperialism and the drive to project national imaginaries that lauded the colonial enterprise. Because it was committed to combine narrative and spectacle to tell the story of colonialism from the colonizer's perspective, cinema tended to speak for the "winners" of history (19). And it is this vantage point that *Raíces Eternas*, a self-proclaimed tribute to the five hundredth anniversary of the "discovery" of Puerto Rico, adopts and proffers. While the individual hero of the film is, indisputably, Cristobal Colón, the collective hero is the assimilated Puerto Rican who finds redemption in his Hispanic ancestry, vows his loyalty to the "motherland," and proclaims his faith to the Catholic Church. In this sense, *Raíces Eternas* is also a project of history.

To view the documentary genre as a project of history is to regard it not just as a reconstruction, however partial or motivated, of the past, but also as an intervention in the present, a scheme for apprehending and acting in current times. Nichols contends that the explanatory framework within which the past is constructed and narrated in the documentary provides "strategies of containment." These strategies account for historical reality by "giving reality the shape of a narrative . . . by proposing a dominant concept, be it narrative closure, teleological destiny, structuring cause or grand theory around which the historical realm can be made known" ("Representing" 143). Seeing it through this lens, we could argue that *Raíces Eternas* strives to muffle the tensions and contradictions of the collective chronicle with the honorable ribbon of national unification and consummation. But taking Nichols's argument a step further, we could also contend that these narrative maneuvers do not simply manage to contain the past; they also impinge upon the present and influence the ongoing process of making history.

The dominant concept of harmonious and conclusive fusion in *Raíces Eternas*, shored up by the grand theory of the melting pot, is intent on promoting a particular subject position for the historical actors who have benefited the least from this ideology. I am referring specifically to women and Afro-Puerto Ricans.

With regards to the first group, the documentary evokes the 19th-century literary trope in which the feminine subject (*la mujer*) stands as the symbol of the homeland (*la patria*). *Raíces Eternas*, however, downplays the *criolla* who inspired the first national literary movement in favor of the Taína. The opening segment of the film allegorically establishes this homology.

The narrator recounts the story of an "*india*," whom the Spanish colonizers "rescue" from a neighboring Antillean Island. She claims to belong to *Boriquén* and readily puts the adventurers to sea in search of her homeland, a quest that fuels their zest to spread the Catholic faith in the New World. The crew's arrival in Puerto Rico is portentously represented in a sequence that intercuts images of the naked Taína running across the splendid seashore and breaking through the pristine wilderness with low-angle shots of the startled but intractable *conquistadores* making their way into the Island as they follow the "*india*," who "escaped once she caught a glimpse of her homeland." The soundtrack provides poignant cues to elucidate the meaning of the images, dispatching a series of signifiers that manage to homologize *la mujer* and *la patria*. First, nondiegetic music is used to christen, so to speak, the hitherto anonymous Taína: a harmonious chorus chants "Boriquén, Boriquén, Boriquén" as we see the character first in a close-up and then in an aerial long-take traversing the seashore. Then, safeguarded by his cross-carrying entourage, Cristóbal Colón solemnly pulls out his sword and firmly presses it into the virginal land. The narrator proclaims: "In the name of Spain and Christ, Boriquén is now San Juan Bautista."[10] This renaming, symbolized with the phallic penetration of the land by the Spanish patriarch, synecdochically furthers the fusion between woman and homeland. In the closing scene of the segment, this union is unequivocally sexualized. After it has been established that the expedition's survival depends on the explorer's ability to find water, the Taína reappears. Her alleged flight has actually led the men to an enchanting "*ojo de agua*" (waterfall); her seductive gaze meets Colón's, who reciprocates when she offers him her water-filled cupped hands. The narrator predicates the exchange as a "mutual process of discovery" between two ancient cultural roots.

In sum, then, the foundation of the historical account produced by *Raíces Eternas* is a particular female subjectivity. It is the native woman who, first, seeks the protection of the Spanish colonizers; then, maps out their path to the exploration and penetration of the Island; and eventually offers them the vital fluid that would guarantee their survival. The savagely docile Taína tenders

---

[10] *Boriquén, ahora para España y para Cristo, es San Juan Bautista.*

herself to the Spanish, an allegory for the volitional submission of the paradisiacal colony. It should be noted, however, that in the fourth segment of the film, the *criolla* subsequently picks up where the Taína left off. She is cast as the fervent upholder and transmitter of patriarchal, Christian and colonial work ethics that guaranteed the stability of the Spanish regime and reproduced its logic in the domestic realm.

In light of what has been said, I would argue that as a project of history—as a scheme for the present—the documentary enunciates, endorses and enjoins a subaltern female subject position. The "eternal roots" of her femininity are lodged in her willingness to consent, facilitate and support the status quo. The female subject rises as a Puerto Rican national insofar as she submits herself to the conquest of the ruling patriarchs, and puts her productive and reproductive labor to the service of their integrationist nationalistic interests.

On the other hand, the film's construction of the Afro-Puerto Rican subject is persistently masculinized. He is the "*negro africano*," whose entry into the national chronicle is attributed to his physical prowess. Though this attribute is emphasized verbally and visually (with lingering shots of muscular black male torsos), he is ultimately corralled into the figure of the redeemed victim. The two scenes that make up the third segment of the film, which attempts to recount the "arrival" of the African slaves in Puerto Rico, poignantly establish his victim status. The first scene tracks a cluster of shackled black males as they are shepherded through an open field to meet their master and face his scrutinizing gaze. The narration anchors the meaning of the image by stating that "*el negro*" came to the New World to play a servile role and be sold like cattle by the European. But the voice-over also serves what Barthes calls a "relay function," setting out meanings that are not to be found in the image itself (41). The *voice of God* explains that the farming and mining economic activities of the colonial period called for a rugged workforce that could bear the hardship of the task and withstand the adverse Antillean climate. On the other hand, the second scene of the segment is a highly dramatized and impeccably shot reconstruction of the branding of a slave with the *carimbo*. The connotations of the colonial practice are fixed for the audience with an ominous pronouncement: "Pain and injustice are the basic elements of black history in Puerto Rican culture."[11]

As we have seen, then, in the only film segment fully devoted to the Afro-Puerto Rican subject, forced labor and physical torture are isolated as his most significant contribution to the collective, national history. The so-called "African presence" during slavery and the colonial period is discursively fettered to the mine and the sugarcane field. Under such circumscription, the

---

[11] *Dolor e injusticia son elementos básicos en la trayectoria histórica del negro en la cultura puertorriqueña.*

carimbo comes to signify less a brand of ownership than an indelible mark of the African's alien(ated) status. However, when "*el negro*" reemerges in the last segment of the film (set in 1986) we are reassured that in contemporary times he is no longer alien(ated) because he is no longer African. "*El negro*" is now *puertorriqueño* because Puerto Rico, to achieve the nation-building mission, has opened itself up to incorporate him.

In the additive rhetoric of *Raíces Eternas*, the Afro-Puerto Rican's legacy to the national character is his endurance of forced labor and physical torture, i.e. his victim status. Needless to say, this representation eclipses the oppositional, resistive and counterhegemonic dimensions of the African presence in Puerto Rico. In so doing, I insist, the documentary seeks to provide a structure to resignify, contain and forge the present. Redemption is the trope it employs to meet this end, elevating "*el negro*" from the status of alien(ated) victim to that of incorporated "Other." The contemporary counter-image of the enchained black male is a self-contented, officially-cloaked black policeman. As the camera tilts up from a close-up of his handgun to a shot of his confident face, we hear the *voice of God* proclaim: "Against the injustices of the past, Puerto Rico opens itself up, reaches out, and takes to its bosom those who were reviled because of the color of their skin and who forge with their labor our reality as a people. . ."[12]

It is this subject position of willful and grateful assimilation that the documentary constructs and offers to contemporary *afropuertorriqueños*. To put it concisely, the documentary's proposal for making history in the present is to silence, or perhaps conquer, the differences and dissent that cast doubt on the myth of the integrated and homogenous nation.

In the preceding pages I have contended that the documentary is not just a purveyor of history but also an intervention in the making of history. The social agents it addresses as both characters and audiences are diligently appropriated by the documentary project with the purpose of bringing the past to bear in the present. However, we should not lose sight of the fact that they/we also appropriate these projections in the process of confronting, living and making our collective histories. This appropriation, the reading of the text, activates both individual and collective memories. In this respect, *Raíces Eternas* is a significant contribution to the process of narrating and making Puerto Rican history. Its strategies of containment are assiduous, yet they insidiously open a space for reconsidering history and reflecting on the conditions that produce its narrativization. This set of circumstances forces us to take stock of the material and symbolic structures that shape our representational endeavors and, to

---

[12] *Ante las injusticias del pasado, Puerto Rico se abre y se incorpora; acoge en su seno a aquellos que fueron agraviados por el color de su piel y que forjan con su frente nuestra realidad de pueblo . . .*

paraphrase Stuart Hall, partake in the "production" of our collective, cultural identity (220).[13] These are indeed the excesses of the documentary project: the narrative closure of the text cannot enclose the workings of memory, the active process of evoking experience and reclaiming the past in the present, reconceiving yesterday in light of today. True: memories are no more "real" or "authentic" than documentary representations. But they are ours, fluid and constantly in the making.

Works Cited

Barthes, Roland. *Image, Music, Text*. Trans. Stephen Heath. New York: Noonday Press, 1977.

Borges, Norma. "Una aportación fílmica a nuestra cultura." *El Mundo* 15 May 1986: 62-63.

Coles, Robert. *Doing Documentary Work*. New York & Oxford: Oxford University Press, 1997.

Fanon, Frantz. *Black Skin, White Masks*. New York: Grove Weidenfeld, 1967.

Hall, Stuart. "Cultural Identity and Cinematic Representation." *Ex-Iles: Essays on Caribbean Cinema*. Ed. Mbye Cham. Trenton: Africa World Press, 1992. 220-236.

Lagny, Michele. *Cine e Historia. Problemas y Métodos en la Investigación Cinematográfica*. Trans. José Luis Fecé. Barcelona: Bosch Casas Editorial, 1997.

Nichols, Bill. *Representing Reality*. Bloomington & Indianapolis: Indiana University Press, 1991.

—."The Voice of Documentary." *New Challenges for Documentary*. Ed. Alan Rosenthal. Berkeley: University of California Press, 1988. 48-63.

Rabiger, Michael. *Directing the Documentary*. Boston & London: Focal Press, 1987.

Raíces Eternas. Dir. Noel Quiñones. Noel Quiñones & Associates, 1985.

Scott, William. *Documentary Expression and Thirties America*. Chicago: University of Chicago Press, 1986.

Stam, Robert. *Film Theory: An Introduction*. Malden & Oxford: Blackwell Publishers, 2000.

Thompson, Kristin, and David Bordwell. *Film History: An Introduction*. 2nd ed. New York: McGraw-Hill, 2003.

---

[13] For Hall, cinematic discourse does not simply represent cultural identity, as though it were an accomplished historical fact, but actually partakes in its production by projecting "different parts and histories of ourselves" and constructing multiple points of identification (220, 236).

Wagenheim, Kal, and Olga Jiménez de Wagenheim, eds. *The Puerto Ricans: A Documentary Project*. Princeton and New York: Markus Weiner Publishers, 1994.

Winston, Brian. "The Tradition of the Victim in Griersonian Documentary." *New Challenges for Documentary*. Ed. Alan Rosenthal. Berkeley: University of California Press, 1988. 269-287.

Zervigón, Pedro. "'*Raíces eternas*': Quinientos años de historia y una nueva raza." *El Reportero* 7 May 1986: 27.

THE JAMAICAN BEGINNINGS
AND WORLD TRAVELS OF CLAUDE MCKAY:
A SEARCH FOR JUSTICE AND EQUALITY

TATIANA TAGIROVA

It is at the heart of national consciousness that international consciousness lives and grows.

Frantz Fanon, *The Wretched of the Earth*

Indeed, the interplay between nationalism and exile is like Hegel's dialectic of servant and master, opposites informing and constituting each other. All nationalisms in their early stages develop from a condition of estrangement.

Edward Said, "Reflections on Exile"

Like a multicolored shell that enables an ear to hear the noise of the ocean, the voice of the human ocean—the hundreds of millions of people liberated from colonialism—is heard in the talented poetry of the big and the smallest West Indian islands.

E. L. Gal'perina, *The Time of Flamboyant Trees: The Poets of the Antillean Islands* (translation mine)

A Long Way from Home (1937) and *My Green Hills of Jamaica* (published posthumously in 1979), two autobiographies by Claude McKay, reveal and illuminate many aspects of his poems, novels and short stories. Therefore, for a proper understanding of his work, they should not be ignored. While *A Long Way from Home* focuses on his international experiences, *My Green Hills of Jamaica* reveals his Jamaican inspiration. The title of *A Long Way From Home* is taken from a Negro spiritual, the opening line of which is, "Sometimes I feel like a motherless child, a long way from home" (LeSeur 300). Yet the man of motion that is seen in McKay's first autobiography is neither a representation of the "rootless drifter" that one finds in Kamau Brathwaite's *Rights of Passage* nor a depiction of V.S. Naipaul's quester for "a place of identification" (Pouchet Paquet 96). Instead, his worldwide travels play a significant role in the formation of a national consciousness shaped by his engagement with the important political and social issues of the twentieth century. As such, the journey provides McKay with an opportunity to express the international consciousness of the black diaspora as he does in *Home to Harlem* (1928) and *Banjo* (1929), the novels he wrote in Europe. However, in *Gingertown* (1932) and *Banana Bottom* (1933), his subsequent works written in Africa, he returns to the Jamaican landscape and its people. *My Green Hills of Jamaica*, then, can be read as a "sequel" to *A Long Way from Home* that shows "the limitations of the vagabond as a sign of identification" and favors a "native space as imaginative home and enabling ground" (Pouchet Paquet 110). Whereas in his first autobiography, *Home to Harlem*, and *Banjo* McKay attempts to reconcile his internationalism with his desire for cultural belonging, in his Jamaican poetry, his second autobiography, and his poetry and narrative devoted to his homeland, he shows his ultimate preference for a national identification. Therefore, Jamaica is indeed a starting and an ending point for the writer and one of the determining influences that shaped his literary formation.

McKay's literary career began in his homeland with *Songs of Jamaica* and *Constab Ballads*, two volumes of poetry in the Jamaican Creole that he published in 1912. The use of such West African loan words as "quashie" and "buccra" in his early poems illuminates his understanding of a complexity of a Jamaican identity influenced by foreign culture and traditions. Both white British aristocrats and poor black Jamaican peasants comprise native culture that he describes. Quashie and buccra are "antipodes of Jamaica's social world: the blackcountry bumpkin, the peasant, the subaltern, and the symbol of power, superordination, the oppressor, the white man" (James 59). The poet's sympathy is clearly with the poor Jamaicans whose voice is heard in his poetry. In "Quashie to Buccra," for example, the Jamaican peasant condemns the insensitive British ruler who takes advantage of his hard work:

> You tas'e petater an' you say it sweet,
> But you no know how hard we wuk fe it;
> You want a basketful fe quattiewut,
> 'Cause you no know how 'tiff de bush fe cut. (*SJ* 13)[1]

---

[1] Claude McKay, *Songs of Jamaica* in *The Dialect Poetry of Claude McKay* (Plainview, New York: Books for Libraries, 1972); hereafter cited parenthetically as *SJ*.

The poem is written from the perspective of a Jamaican of rural, peasant origin who resists colonial exploitation. Sweet potatoes are a product that rich whites consume without thinking about the hard labor that the peasants put into its cultivation (James 60). Buccra wants to buy potatoes for the cheapest possible price because he is not the one who actually has to grow the crop. Therefore, he does not understand its real worth. The peasant does all the hard work, yet he is not able to fully enjoy the fruits of his labor. As this poem demonstrates, there is a gap between the acts of production and consumption as a result of which the peasants become estranged from consumers (James 60).

In addition to being an exploiter who takes advantage of the peasants' labor, buccra is also an educator who wants to impose his knowledge and culture on the natives. This domineering teacher appears in the poem "Cudjoe Fresh From De Lecture" where McKay describes him as an instructor who wants to enlighten the peasants:

'Top one minute, Cous' Jarge, an' sit do'n 'pon
    de grass,
An' mek a tell you 'bout de news I hear at las',
How de buccra te-day tek time an' begin teach
All of us dat was deh in a clear open speech. (*SJ* 55)

As the buccra goes on with his teaching concerning creation, civilization, and progress, he states that if the Jamaican natives were to continue to live in Africa, they would be "maybe same half-naked—all day dribe buccra cow, / an' tearin' t'rough de bush wid all de monkey dem, / wile an' uncibilise', an' neber comin' tame" (*SJ* 57). This kind of teaching upsets Cudjoe and he runs away from this lecture. However, he can't run too far because everywhere he goes he encounters his teacher: "Yet both horse partly runnin' in de selfsame gallop, / For it is nearly so de way de buccra pull up" (*SJ* 58). The native is trapped in the ideas, culture and the exploitation of the British ruler. In spite of this, however, he does not concede to the racist philosophy of his instructor. On the contrary, he contests the buccra's instruction and takes pride in his Afro-Jamaican heritage in "My Native Land, My Home":

Jamaica is de nigger's place,
    No mind whe' some declare;
Although dem call we "no-land race,"
    I know we home is here....
You draw de t'ousan' from deir shore,
    An' all 'long keep dem please';
De invalid come here fe cure,
    You heal all deir disease.... (*SJ* 84-85)

This is the poet's homeland, a wonderful country with rich culture and traditions that has the potential to bring happiness and tranquility to its people. However, these blessing cannot come forth because "buccra 'poil de whole / wid gove'mint an' all de res, / fworry naygur soul" (*SJ* 85). In this poem the narrator contests buccra's previous teaching of superiority and accuses him of diminishing his homeland.

McKay's devotion to the oppressed blacks articulated in *Songs of Jamaica* is further developed in *Constab Ballads*. The poet's experience in urban Kingston's constabulary made him even more aware of the broad gap that existed between most black Jamaicans and their British rulers (Cooper 37). Most of the poems are directed against the Kingston policeman, "a hated 'red seam,' as the peasants alluding to their uniform, derisively dubbed members of the constabulary" (James 71). In "The Apple-Woman's Complaint" McKay criticizes a policeman who stops a woman from selling her apples:

> While me deh walk 'long in de street,
> Policeman's yawnin'on his beat;
> An' dis de wud him chiefta'n say-
> Me mus'n' car' me apply-tray. (*CB* 57)[2]

The thoughtless policeman doesn't care that selling apples is the woman's only means of earning a living. By stopping her from doing it, he complicates her life:

> Ef me no wuk, me boun' fe tief;
> S'pose dat will please de police chief!
> De prison dem mus' be wan' full,
> Mek dem's 'pon we like ravin' bull....
>
> Dem wan' fe see we in de street
> Dah foller dem all 'pon dem beat;
> An' after, 'dout a drop o' shame,
> Say we be'n dah solicit dem. (*CB* 57-58)

McKay describes a cruel world in which the justice system does not protect the poor woman's rights but works against her. Instead of finding means to receive a reward for her labor, she encounters apathy and distress. She feels helpless before the selfish, uncaring policeman who wants to force the woman into committing a crime so he can put her in jail. In her desperate cry, she asks Jesus

---

[2] Claude McKay, *Constab Ballads* in *The Dialect Poetry of Claude McKay* (Plainview, New York: Books for Libraries, 1972); hereafter cited parenthetically as *CB*.

to show her how she can live an honest life in the unjust world that surrounds her:

O massa Jesus! Don't you see
How police is oppressin' we?...

Ah massa Jesus! in you' love
Jes' look do'n from you' t'rone above,
An' show me how a poo' weak gal
Can lib good life in dis ya wul'. (*CB* 58)

In "The Apple-Woman's Complaint," described as "one of the most sorrowful and desperate of McKay's early poems," the poet not only shows his protest against the oppression of women, but also illustrates that "complaint of the powerless, the heedless voice of one of the little people, the wailing of the condemned" is not heard (James 108).

Even though in 1910 McKay himself became a policeman, later on he left this profession because he understood its unworthiness. As Wayne Cooper notes, the poet's duties as a "constab" made him stress his "fundamental identity as a black man and to reaffirm his peasant origins" (42). His association with the black masses of Jamaica and his preference for the country life is clearly seen in "The Heart of a Constab," a poem in which he expresses his feelings of regret through the policeman-narrator:

'Tis hatred without an' 'tis hatred within,
        An' I am so weary an' sad;
For all t'rough de tempest o' terrible strife
        Dere's not'in' to make poor me glad...

Oh ! what have I gained from my too too rash act
        O' joinin' a hard Constab Force,
Save quenchin' me thirst from a vinegar cup,
        De vinegar cup o' remorse ?...

But I'll leave it, my people, an' come back to you,
        I'll flee from de grief an' turmoil;
I'll leave it, though flow'rs here should line my
        path yet,
An' come back to you an' de soil. (*CB* 62-63)

The policeman wants to return to "my people, my people, me owna black skin" and vows to never depart again from the country that he deeply loves (*CB* 63). The feelings of the narrator echo those of McKay who in "A Negro Poet Writes" stated that he "joined the Jamaican Constabulary... despised it and left" (276).

His own distressing experience as a Kingston policeman served as a strategic move in the formation of "an openly black nationalist position where he felt part of the black masses of his Jamaica" (James 72).

McKay's inclination to rebel against injustices manifested in *Songs of Jamaica* and *Constab Ballads* increased in the United States. In October of 1917, *Seven Arts* published "Invocation" and "The Harlem Dancer," two sonnets whose "lyric forms, though traditional, expressed the spirit and consciousness of black America and uncovered the muffled voice of ancient Africa" (Cooper 81). In "Invocation" McKay appeals to his African roots, which had been demolished by colonialism and the hegemony of European civilization:

> Bring ancient music to my modern heart,
> Let fall the light upon my sable face
> That once gleamed upon the Ethiopian's art,
> Lift me to thee out of this alien place
> So I may be, thine exiled counterpart,
> The worthy singer of my world and race. (*CP* 132)[3]

He was well familiar with the massive scattering of millions of men and women out of their African homes and the misery of Caribbean and African American people as a result of this separation. In "McKay's Human Pity: A Note on His Poetry," Arthur D. Drayton argues that it is not surprising that he won recognition through his verse written around the theme of Negro suffering in the States. In his opinion, as a Caribbean writer, McKay "was fired by what he saw in the States and helped to give to American Negro poetry a distinctly different voice" (40). In his American poems, he not only condemned racial injustices, but also "renounced the entire social, economic, and political order that had allowed these injustices to occur" (Cooper 101).

If in 1917 McKay turned to Africa in search of his own as well as African American identity, by the spring of 1919 he was ready "to proclaim his own political militancy and to plunge into the turbulent, exhilarating waters of revolutionary politics and art" (Cooper 99). This he did through the publication of his poems in *Liberator*, a magazine where he could both promote the cause of social justice and find himself as a writer and artist. His famous poem "If We Must Die," which "exploded" out of the poet (*LW* 31),[4] became a call to African Americans to stand brave before their white oppressors:

---

[3] Claude McKay, *Complete Poems* (Urbana and Chicago: University of Illinois Press, 2004); hereafter cited parenthetically as *CP*.

[4] Claude McKay, *A Long Way from Home* (San Diego, New York, London: Harcourt, Brace Jovanovich, 1970); hereafter cited parenthetically as *LW*.

If we must die, let it not be like hogs
Hunted and penned in an inglorious spot,
While round us bark the mad and hungry dogs,
Making their mock at our accursed lot.
If we must die, O let us nobly die,
So that our precious blood may not be shed
In vain; then even the monsters we defy
Shall be constrained to honor us though dead!
O kinsmen! we must meet the common foe!
Though far outnumbered let us show us brave,
And for their thousand blows deal one deathblow!
What though before us lies the open grave?
Like men we'll face the murderous, cowardly pack,
Pressed to the wall, dying, but fighting back! (*CP* 177-178)

As George Kent accurately observes in his article "The Soulful Way of Claude McKay," the poem came at a time when Black people needed it most for their "shaken morale" (42). It was immediately reprinted in black newspapers and magazines and gained the attention of a black audience whose "deep emotions and post-World War I spirit of defiance were at the heart of its defiant lines" (Kent 38). It condemned violence against black people, and called upon them to resist the murderers with courage. With the appearance of "If We Must Die," the Negro people unanimously declared him a poet (*LW* 31). At the moment of writing, McKay was not aware that he "was transformed into a medium to express a mass sentiment" (*LW* 228). The mighty voice of "a high-spirited and cultivated Black man" fused with "the rage of his people" (Kent 43).

While, according to McKay, Jamaica was "too small for high achievement" (*LW* 20), there was tremendous prejudice toward the black writer in the United States at the beginning of the twentieth century. In their article "A Black Briton Comes Home," Wayne Cooper and Robert Reinders affirm that two years in America taught McKay "how completely his race was being exploited" (68). In light of his experience, it is not surprising that he became associated with and was influenced by several West Indian radicals who "combined an interest in socialism with an ardent zeal for Negro rights" (Cooper and Reinders 68). Even though McKay was not a follower of Marcus Garvey since he considered his teachings to be "too bourgeois," like Garvey he "proved an innovator" (68-69). Through his tense and angry sonnets he "injected a new aggressiveness into Negro American literature" (Cooper and Reinders 69).

After the publication of his poems in *Liberator* and becoming "a militant black poet" in New York (Cooper 108), McKay continued his world travels. He spent seven years in America and arrived in England in the fall of 1919. Like the United States, it became a site of political and professional growth as a well as a place where he could not find justice and equality. He found London to be a "harshly unfriendly" city filled with "a strangely unsympathetic people, as coldly chilling as their English fog" (*LW* 67). McKay probably expected racial discrimination in England to be like the one found in Jamaica, but instead he discovered that English were "not much more tolerant" than Americans (Cooper and Reinders 80). In *A Long Way From Home*, he admits he wouldn't have survived more than a year in London if he hadn't come in contact with a club for "colored soldiers" and the International Club he attended (67-68).

At these clubs McKay not only listened to the stories of black soldiers from the West Indies, Egypt and other countries about their war experiences in France, Egypt and Arabia, but he also introduced them to the ideas of the "American Negroes" of that time (*LW* 67). There he got to know Polish, Russian, and German Jews, Czechs, Italians, and Irish nationalists (*LW* 68). The writer's contact with the International Club "stimulated and broadened" his social outlook and "plunged" him into the reading of Karl Marx (*LW* 68). While there was "no romance" for him in London, there was "plenty of radical knowledge" (*LW* 68). Marxist debates that took place at the International Club introduced him to the world of England's political Left (Cooper 111). His subsequent meeting of Sylvia Pankhurst and an involvement with her newspaper, *Workers' Dreadnought*, placed him in the midst of British socialists (Cooper 114).

England provided McKay with an opportunity to publish *Spring in New Hampshire*, the book of poetry in which he expresses nostalgia for his homeland. While living in London in 1920, McKay wrote "I Shall Return," a poem that shows Jamaica's special place in his heart and mind that none of the other new and interesting places could fill:

> I shall return to loiter by the streams
> That bathe the brown blades of the bending grasses,
> And realize once more my thousand dreams
> Of waters rushing down the mountain passes.
> I shall return to hear the fiddle and fife
> Of village dances, dear delicious tunes
> That stir the hidden depth of native life,
> Stray melodies of dim remembered runes.
> I shall return. I shall return again,
> To ease my mind of long, long years of pain. (*CP* 167-168)

After several years of separation from Jamaica, McKay remembers it fondly and hopes to return one day to a country that can cure his emptiness and hurt. The poem shows love, longing, and patriotism for Jamaica that is "not adulterated with imperial sentiments" (Oakley 92).

In the writer's most difficult moments abroad, he took refuge in his memory and found "an ideal and positive source of joy" in the celebration of his birthplace (Hansell 7). "Flame Heart," a poem in which he describes Jamaica's splendor and lure, is one of such examples:

> So much I have forgotten in ten years,
>   So much in ten brief years! I have forgot
> What time the purple apples come to juice,
>   And what month brings the shy forget-me-not.
> I have forgot the special, startling season
>   Of the pimento's flowering and fruiting;
> What time of year the ground doves brown the fields
>   And fill the noonday with their curious fluting.
> I have forgotten much, but still remember
> The poinsettia's red, blood-red, in warm December. (*CP* 155)

His description of "purple apples," "forget-me-not," and "the pimento's flowering and fruiting" show Jamaica as a beautiful and charming place. This poem is "a sort of nostalgia for home, for relatives, and for the scenes of childhood days, long past" (Smith 272). It creates a feeling of serenity and peace that he can find only in Jamaica, a country that provides for the writer "the sense of belonging to a unified and harmonious way of life" (Hansell 9). Gayle insightfully observes that in spirit, McKay goes back to "his own Garden of Eden, uncorrupted by Western technology and industrialization—a land where emotions took precedence over cold, calculating reason, where nature reigned, not red in tooth and claw, but tenderly and benevolently" (22).

Despite the nostalgic feelings for Jamaica that "I Shall Return," and "Flame-Heart" reveal, McKay did not go back to his homeland after his sojourn in England. However, his experience in Great Britain "seriously weakened his identification with western Caucasian values" (Cooper and Reinders 80-81). Disappointed with England and the English, he returned to the United States in 1921 (Cooper 126). There he resumed his association with *Liberator* and continued to contribute articles, book reviews and poems to one of the most radical magazines in the United States that was "far ahead of most white magazines in recognizing the importance of the challenge African-American history posed to the myths of white America" (Hutchinson 250). During that time he composed "his most significant American poetry," which represented his "mature understanding of the black dilemma in Western culture" (Cooper 151). *Harlem Shadows*, the book of poetry he published in the United States, uplifted him with "the greatest joy" of his life experience (*LW* 148). The anger and alienation that McKay felt in an unfair world dominated by the whites, the world in which the black race was denied humanity, justice, and equality, found an expression in this book. In "Outcast" he condemns the Western civilization that separated him from his roots:

> ...Something in me is lost, forever lost,
> Some vital thing has gone out of my heart,
> And I must walk the way of life a ghost
> Among the sons of earth, a thing apart;
> For I was born, far from my native clime,
> Under the white man's menace, out of time. (*CP* 174)

The narrator of the poem contests the greatness of this civilization and shows the negative effects of colonialism that make him feel at a loss. The capitalism and the colonialism that took Africans away from their native land is also the reason workers dread a coming dawn in the poem "The Tired Worker":

> The wretched day was theirs, the night is mine;
> Come tender sleep, and fold me to thy breast.
> But what steals out the gray clouds red like wine?
> O dawn! O dreaded dawn! O let me rest
> Weary my veins, my brain, my life! Have pity!
> No! Once again the harsh, the ugly city. (*CP* 173)

The poems of *Harlem Shadows* in which McKay speaks on behalf of "millions of black Americans" fighting against racism and inequality represent a "new poetical school" and constitute an "important chapter of the American history of the twentieth century" (Zverev 24-25) (translation mine).

After the publication of *Harlem Shadows*, McKay decided to visit the Soviet Union and to see for himself the results of the 1917 revolution. Russia "signaled" and he responded in search of new understanding and knowledge for his life and work:

> Go and see, was the command. Escape from the pit of sex and poverty, from
> domestic death, from the cul-de-sac of self-pity, from the hot syncopated
> fascination of Harlem, from the suffocating ghetto of color consciousness. Go,
> better than stand still, keep going. (*LW* 150)

According to Cooper, in 1922 McKay left for Russia in the hope that he would find evidence that "the equality, justice, freedom, and humane treatment of his fellow men he had envisioned under socialism was actually taking place" (170). Even though he attended the Fourth Congress of the Communist International, he was not invited by the Soviet government nor was he sent by the American Communist Party (*LW* 153). All he had was "the dominant urge to go" that "discovered the way" (*LW* 153).

Despite the efforts of American communists to prevent him from attending the conference, the poet won the right of "a special delegate" (Cooper 173-174). His vindication resulted from two sources. First, Sen Katayama, the leading Japanese Communist at the Fourth Congress of Comintern, confirmed McKay's knowledge of the black masses and convinced Comintern officials that the poet could speak authoritatively about the potential role of blacks in the international Communist movement. Second, the Russian people on the streets found his color, height, smile, and laughter to be attractive (Cooper 174). As McKay writes:

> Never before had I experienced such an instinctive sentiment of affectionate feeling compelling me to the bosom of any people, white or colored. And I am certain I never will again. My response was as sincere as the mass feeling was spontaneous. That miraculous experience was so extraordinary that I have never been able to understand it. (*LW* 167)

As "the first Negro to arrive in Russia since the revolution," he considered himself to be a "black ikon in the flesh" and "an omen of good luck" (*LW* 168). Never in his life had he felt prouder of "being an African, a black" for from Moscow to Petrograd and from Petrograd to Moscow he went "triumphantly from surprise to surprise" (*LW* 168). Even the bourgeois were interested in his poetry. As a token of appreciation for him as a poet, the anti-Bolshevik Russian professor and "old classic scholar" who worshiped Pushkin's books gave McKay a photograph of the Russian poet as a young boy with clearly seen Negroid features. Throughout his life he thought of this portrait as one of the few most precious treasures of his life (*LW* 169-170).[5]

Even though he had a great desire to attend the Congress and to see for himself the new life of the Soviet Union, he admitted that he could be neither a politician, for he was "temperamentally unfit" for this role, nor "a disciplined member of any Communist party," for he was "born to be a poet" (*LW* 173). Despite the writer's opinion of himself as "merely a poet" (*LW* 179), however, McKay's account of his participation in the proceedings of the congress is to some extent misleading. According to Cooper, in *A Long Way From Home* he failed to acknowledge the fact that he spoke as both a black Communist and a black writer who wanted the Soviet government to understand the role of blacks within the international Communist movement:

---

[5] I found this portrait in the James Weldon Johnson Collection of Negro Literature and Art, the Yale Collection of American Literature, the Beinecke Rare Book and Manuscript Library during my doctoral research in the summer of 2004.

By the time he got to Moscow, McKay had grown skeptical about the
willingness or ability of his white comrades in England or America to embrace
blacks as true equals within the movement. The Comintern provided him a
platform to relate his experiences and explain his perspective, and he took full
advantage of the opportunity; he had, in fact, come to Moscow primed to attack
American Communists for their reluctance to deal with the race problem. (175)

McKay, "a vagabond with a purpose" (*LW* 4), didn't go to Russia just to see
what he could learn for his life and work; he also went there to tell the Russians
about the conditions of American Negroes and to share with them the racist
attitudes of American Communists towards them. He contributed tremendously
towards the Soviet understanding of the Negro problem though his Soviet
publications for which he was paid as a literary celebrity, as an important writer
called *bolshoi* (big) by one of the Russian journalists:

> That, *bolshoi! bolshoi! bolshoi!* (big! big! big!) was sweet music in my ears and
> an inspiration. But it also stirred up a hell of discontent within me. Why should I
> be "big" translated into Russian?…I felt that if I were to be *bolshoi* as a literary
> artist in a foreign language, I should first make a signal achievement in my
> native adopted language, English. (*LW* 186)

In *Negroes in America*, the book published in Russia in 1923, he presents an
analysis of African American conditions in North America at the beginning of
the twentieth century. In addition to a Marxist interpretation of black American
history, a discussion of the economic basis of race relations in the United States,
and a criticism of the Communist outlook and approach toward blacks since
World War I (Cooper 185), he also addresses exploitation based on gender that
he finds to be similar to that of race and class. [6]

By going to the Soviet Union, the writer joined other black and white
American radicals who looked to the Bolshevik Revolution as "an example of
how to achieve the unfulfilled democratic promises of the 'old regimes'
throughout Europe and America" (Cooper 101). His longing to see a Western
civilization in which both black and white people could live in dignity and
freedom as well as his condemnation of white America was justified by a belief
that a future social system must be dedicated to the worker, not the capitalist
(Cooper 101). McKay believed in a social system in which "black and white
laborers would no longer have to compete for the 'almighty dollar' but could
work together for a classless society" (Cooper 101). In spite of this, however, he
never totally committed himself to the Soviet ideology. As he writes to James

---

[6] McKay further fictionally develops his theoretical claim on the interrelationship
between race, class, and sex in *Trial by Lynching: Stories about Negro life in North
America*, another Soviet publication that followed *The Negroes in America*.

Weldon Johnson in a letter dated May 8, 1935, he went to Russia as "a writer and a free spirit" and he left the same (*CMPJ 4-119*)).[7] Even though he enjoyed a warm personal acceptance and appreciation by the Russians, he had a greater desire:

> I left Russia with one determination and one objective: to write. I was not received in Russia as a politician, but primarily as a Negro poet. And the tremendous reception was a great inspiration and urge to write more. I often felt in Russia that I was honored as a poet altogether out of proportion to my actual performance. And thus I was fired with the desire to accomplish the utmost. (*LW* 226)

When McKay left Russia, he was "determined to write at all costs" as long as he had a piece of bread and a room in which he could "think and scribble" (*LW* 229). His triumphant experience in Russia paved his longing to be a "great artist, a spokesperson for his own people" (Baldwin 84).

After Russia and a brief visit to Germany in the fall of 1923, he journeyed to Paris, an emerging site of African American intellectual life of that time. In his article "African American and Francophone Black Intellectuals during the Harlem Renaissance," Kenneth Janken writes:

> Further, for the New Negro intellectuals, Paris became a link to African intellectuals of French Africa and the Caribbean. Whether through the Pan-African political movement of the early and mid-1920s that sought equality and opportunity for all those scattered through the African diaspora, or in the black cultural salons of the late 1920s and 1930s, black American intellectuals met face to face with their francophone black counterparts: They became acquainted with each other's condition, fortified themselves with each other's accomplishments, and fostered a diaspora-wide sense of community. (487-8)

It was in Paris that McKay encountered a "novel and elastic" cosmopolitan environment in which "radicals, esthetes, painters and writers, pseudo-artists, bohemian tourists-all mixed tolerantly and congenially enough together" (*LW* 243). "The cream of Harlem," Negro communists going and returning from Russia, and the Negro students from European universities came in contact with each other and expanded their horizons through their interactions (*LW* 311).

---

[7] Claude McKay Papers; James Weldon Johnson Collection of Negro Literature and Art, the Yale Collection of American Literature, the Beinecke Rare Book and Manuscript Library; hereafter cited parenthetically as *CMPJ* and followed by the box and the folder numbers.

France provided McKay with an opportunity to see racism and social injustices similar to the ones that he encountered in the States and England. Even prior to his going there, he understood the reality of French liberalism. In *From Harlem to Paris: Black American Writers in France 1840-1980,* Michel Fabre writes:

> He [McKay] was also quick to denounce French racism. He was convinced that, in spite of appearances, Senegalese Blaise Diagne had undermined W. E. B. Du Bois's efforts at the 1919 Pan-African Conference in Paris: hadn't Diagne declared that French blacks should consider themselves Frenchmen, not colored internationalists, for "the position of Negro citizens in France [was] truly worthy of envy"? Yet even such an active supporter of assimilation as Diagne, McKay noted, had been forced to concede that French whites denied the black man even mere physical equality: the victory of Senegalese boxer Battling Siki over native Frenchman Georges Charpentier for the world championship had created no less a scandal than that of Jack Johnson over Australian Tommy Burns. (93)

In "Once More the Germans Face Black Troops," an article published in *Opportunity* in November of 1939, McKay compares his personal experience in France with that of Germany and favorably speaks of "cordial relationship" between the African troops and the common German people that "appeared even more natural and intimate" than those he observed in France (323). Despite the government's racist agitation against the African troops in the Rhineland, the common German folk demonstrated a positive attitude towards the black soldiers fighting on behalf of France, which "seemed to be the kindliest and most considerate in Europe" ("Once More" 328). Questions such as "Do you like us Germans?" and "Do they like us in America?" which McKay was asked by the Germans amazed him especially when he thought of people in France who would never ask those questions for they believed that "France should be admired by any visitor as the most civilized country in the world" (328). As Fabre notes, McKay not only condemned the French feeling of superiority, but also provided "a sophisticated analysis of race prejudice there and of the pro-French attitude of the gullible Afro-American intelligentsia" and refused to "exonerate French institutions and culture from responsibility for their colonial oppression" (93-94). His subsequent traveling between 1929 and 1931 in Tangier, Madrid, and Paris before settling in an Arab village of Tangier till his return to the United States made him even more aware of French colonialism, and some of his comments anticipated Frantz Fanon's criticism during the Algerian war of independence (Lewis 44).

While the greatest part of *Banjo* was written in Marseilles, by the spring of 1928 the writer had to escape the French port in order to finish it (Cooper 237-

238). Barcelona, a place that took his breath away, became the next abode. In his letters to James Weldon Johnson written between 1928 and 1931, he states:

> Perhaps you know Barcelona—a beautiful city and it is a happy change after France and more to my fancy, but I am working so hard I haven't had a chance to enjoy anything yet.

> If you ever come to Europe soon, you must be sure to visit Spain. I am sure that both you and Mrs. Johnson will be charmed by it. It is the only European country that touches me emotionally. (*CMPJ* 13-38)

Even though he intended to spend just three days in Barcelona when he went there with a Senegalese boxer, he ended up staying for three months (*LW* 295-296).

Following his stay in Spain, McKay accepted "a second invitation" from a Martinican sailor to go to Morocco (*LW* 296), a country that reminded him of his homeland. At the end of September 1928, he visited Casablanca, a place of "the overwhelming European atmosphere" (*LW* 298). After that, he journeyed to Rabat, a "delightfully different city" where "the native life was the big tree with solid roots and spreading branches" (*LW* 298). It provided the ambiance he needed to finish *Banjo*. After that, he "plunged enthusiastically into the life around him" (Cooper 249), going "completely native," and feeling "singularly free of color-consciousness" (*LW* 299-300). In a letter to Max Eastman McKay writes that no place satisfied him as much as Morocco since he had left home for there were "many things in the life of the natives, their customs and superstitions, reminiscent of Jamaica" (Cooper 271). In another letter to W.A. Bradley, he states he was ready to write "the Jamaican book—dealing with the religious customs and social life of the peasants" for he was feeling "very religious" among the Moslems (Cooper 271).

McKay's search for justice and equality was not just geographical. While he spent some time in the United States, England, Soviet Union, France, Spain, and Africa and learned a lot from these "logical steps" of his pilgrimage (letter to James Weldon Johnson dated May 8, 1935, *CMPJ* 4-419), in Morocco he turned to the Moslem religion in his spiritual search for equality between blacks and whites. In another letter to James Weldon Johnson dated May 25, 1931 he adds:

> I am seriously contemplating becoming a Moslem. The social side of the life that is blind to racial and color prejudices appeals to me greatly and as the religion is mostly great poetry, I can conscientiously subscribe to it, as a poet. (*CMPJ* 13-38)

According to Archer Winsten, the author of an article, "In the Wake of the News: Claude McKay Returns to Harlem from Morocco," which appeared in the

New York Evening Post on February 26, 1934, upon his return from Africa
McKay felt as color conscious as he had felt twenty years before when he wrote
his "bitter poems on race questions" (*CMPJ* 15-455). As Winsten adds, unlike
the United States, Morocco gave him "something he had not found in his native
West Indies, not in Harlem and not in France," for the Moslems of Morocco
made him feel completely without color consciousness for the first time in his
life (*CMPJ* 15-455).

The community, solidarity, and sovereignty that McKay found in Africa
inspired him to depict the beauty of the Jamaican countryside in the prose he
wrote there. The African setting encouraged him to fictionally return to a
Jamaican community not only in *Banana Bottom*, but also in *Gingertown* and
My Green Hills of Jamaica, books in which he included "Truant," "The
Agricultural Show, " "Crazy Mary," "When I Pounded the Pavement," and "The
Strange Burial of Sue." All of these stories are somewhat reminiscent of the
writer's experience in his homeland. Even though the setting of "Truant" is New
York, in *My Green Hills of Jamaica* McKay still places it under the title
"Jamaican Short Stories." Barclay, its main character, is a West Indian peasant
boy who feels like a prisoner within "the huge granite-gray walls of New York"
(*G* 152).[8] He nostalgically remembers his native home, as he is trapped in the
intricate life of this city:

> Dreaming of tawny tasseled fields of sugar-cane, and silver-gray John-tuhits
> among clusters of green and glossy-blue berries of pimento. The husbands and
> fathers of his village were not mechanically-driven servant boys. They were
> hardy, independent tillers of the soil or struggling artisans.
> What enchantment had lured him away from the green intimate life that
> clustered round his village—the simple African-transplanted life of the West
> Indian hills? Why had he hankered for the hard-slabbed streets, the vertical
> towns, the gray complex life of this steel-tempered city? Stone and steel! Steel
> and stone! Mounting in heaven-pursuing magnificence. Feet piled upon feet,
> miles circling miles, of steel and stone.... (152)

Barclay feels that he is a slave to New York. Only in moments when he is "lost
in the past" can he remember the sense of freedom that he experienced as a
West Indian peasant. City life intensifies in him the fond memories of his
village:

> Yellow-eyed and white-lidden Spanish needles coloring the grassy hillsides,
> barefooted black girls, straight like young sweet-woods, tramping to market with
> baskets of mangoes or star-apples poised unsupported on their heads. The native

---

[8] Claude McKay, *Gingertown* (NewYork: Harper and Bros., 1932): hereafter cited
parenthetically as *G*.

cockish liquor juice of the sugar-cane, fermented in bamboo joints for all-night carousal at wakes and tea-meeting.... (*G* 159-60)

Whether in New York or Kingston, the city destroys a sense of individuality and personal freedom. Like Barclay, who feels a prisoner of New York, the narrator of "When I Pounded the Pavement" is "the son of peasants" who had grown up in an environment of "individual reserve and initiative" (*G* 208). In Jamaica's capital, he is "thrown among a big depot of men of different character from bush and small town to mix in a common life with them" (208). When the narrator becomes a city constab, he is not happy with this profession because he inherits "the peasant's instinctive hostility for police people" (*G* 211). The policemen of this story are as bad as the insensitive, unkind, and senseless policeman of "The Apple-Woman's Complaint" who doesn't allow the countrywoman to sell her apples. Contrary to the city, McKay's rural Jamaican village with its own rights and regulations is a happier place where one can find a sense of community. For example, in "The Agricultural Show," country people are much more excited about the show than the town people. For them, this event is not just "an agricultural but a community affair" (*G* 168). The writer's retrospective view of Jamaica as a unified, agrarian, and harmonious community becomes an inspirational setting different from that of the previous places.

McKay's international travels and experiences illuminated his understanding of the importance of Negro national consciousness and convinced him that African Americans had to unite and learn how to rely upon themselves in order to achieve their goals. In a letter to James Weldon Johnson dated April 15, 1935 he writes:

> I learned very much abroad, especially in Africa. And I am certain that Negroes will have to realize themselves as an organized group to get anything. Wherever I traveled I observed that the people who were getting anywhere and anything were those who could realize the strength of their cultural groups, their political demands were considered and determined by the force of their cultural grouping: it was the same underlying principle in Communist Russia as in Fascist Spain and democratic France and England and in "protected" Africa. (*CMPJ* 13-38)

In an earlier letter to Max Eastman dated September 1, 1932, he states, "My attachment to Tangier is sort of spiritual looking backwards."[9] His African experience provided "the kind of deep-seated, traditional community self-sufficiency that he had known as a child in the hills of Jamaica" (Cooper 272).

---

[9] Claude McKay's Letters to Max Eastman from 1928 to 1934, The Lilly Library, Indiana University.

He returned to the United States convinced that American blacks could learn a lot from the minority groups in Europe and North Africa:

> In his (McKay's) opinion, international communism had failed, and blacks should concentrate on strengthening their collective group life and promoting democratic government at home in order to be in a position to meet all eventualities. (Cooper 306)

He understood the importance of the Negroes' realization of themselves as an organized, self-sufficient, and self-reliable cultural group as a result of these experiences, especially the one in Morocco. In his letter to James Weldon Johnson dated April 3, 1937, he states that the three years of living in Africa were like "studying three hundred years of life there" (*CMPJ* 13-309). In the same letter, he also criticizes the tactics of orthodox Communists for their "aim to suppress independent thinking and opposition opinion" and as "a member of a minority group which was the age-long victim of intolerance," he refuses to embrace Communist intolerance (*CMPJ* 13-309).

McKay's interest in the Moslem religion as a way to find unity and equality among different racial groups was similar to his attraction to Catholicism, the religion he turned to at the end of his life, for he believed it provided "peace" and "good will on earth" to all kinds of men regardless of their color. In "Right Turn to Catholicism" he writes :

> Jesus Christ rejected the ideal of any special, peculiar or chosen race or nation, when he charged his apostles: Go ye unto all the world and preach the gospel. Not the gospel of Imperialism, Feudalism or Capitalism, or Socialism, Communism or a National Church... I find in the Catholic Church that which doesn't exist in Capitalism, Socialism or Communism–the one true International of Peace and Good Will on earth to all men. (*CMPJ* 9-298)

In another essay, "Why I Became a Catholic," McKay explains the role of "color and race" in his decision to become a Catholic:

> Like the Mohammedan religion today, there never was any race and color prejudice in the Roman Catholic Church from its beginning up until the Reformation.
> It is said that three of the early popes were Negroid. In the Schomburg library in New York there is the photograph of the nephew of a pope–a duke–who is unmistakably Negro....But, as I have said, there was no race or color prejudice in the world of the early church, and so it was not necessary or important to mention the color or race of any of its protagonists. (32)

Even though one may not agree with his assessment of Catholicism, one can "scarcely characterize his conversion as inconsistent with his life" (Hillyer

Condit 357). In the Catholic Church, the writer found "that sense of wholeness very important to him" without a compromise of his individuality (Hillyer Condit 357). At the end of his life, he discovered "a humanism and spirituality" that gave him "inspiration and brotherhood" (Goldweber 13).

To conclude, McKay's autobiographies reveal two sources of his formation. One is that of his connectedness to Jamaica, its culture, and community, and the other is that of his international inspiration. Even though he considered himself to be a "poet without country," someone with an "international mind" (McKay's letter to Langston Hughes, *LHPJ* 109-2042) [10] who was "always obsessed with the idea of universality of life under the different patterns and colors and felt it was altogether too grand to be distorted creatively in the interest of any one group" (McKay's letter to James Weldon Johnson, *CMPJ* 13-30), his deep sense of belonging to the Jamaican community is evident in his narratives. As Cooper accurately observes, in *Banana Bottom*, McKay's final novel written in Morocco, his search for the psychic unity and stability that began in *Home to Harlem*, "came full circle to rest again in the lost paradise of his pastoral childhood" (282). His pioneering articulation of problem of the Jamaican identity found its expression in his writings. While his long travels abroad enabled him to see the black diaspora in a wider perspective, he was to express particular Jamaican issues and concerns in his poetry and prose. His life abroad provided not only material for his literary work, but also exposed him to the major political and social issues of the 1920s and 1930s. As McKay's international consciousness grew as a result of his travels in the United States, England, Russia, Germany, France, Spain, and Morocco, his national Jamaican consciousness also increased.

Works Cited

Baldwin, Kate. *Beyond The Color Line and The Iron Curtain. Reading Encounter Between Black and Red, 1922-1963*. Durham and London: Duke UP, 2002.

Chauhan, P.S. "Rereading Claude McKay." *College Language Association Journal* 34:1 (1996): 68-80.

Cooper, Wayne. *Claude McKay: Rebel Sojourner in the Harlem Renaissance*. Baton Rouge: Louisiana State UP, 1987.

Cooper, Wayne and Robert C. Reiders. "A Black Briton Comes Home." *Race* 9 (1967): 67-83.

---

[10] Langston Hughes Papers, James Weldon Johnson Collection of Negro Literature and Art, the Yale Collection of American Literature, the Beinecke Rare Book and Manuscript Library; followed by the box and the folder numbers.

Drayton, Arthur. "McKay's Human Pity: A Note on His Protest Poetry." *Black Orpheus* 17 (1965): 39-40.

Eastman, Max. "Introduction." *Harlem Shadows: The Poems of Claude McKay.* New York: Harcourt, Brace and Company, 1922. ix-xviii.

Fabre, Michel. *From Harlem to Paris: Black American Writers in France 1840-1980.* U of Illinois P, 1991.

Fanon, Frantz. *The Wretched of the Earth.* New York: Grove Press, 1963.

Gal'perina, E.L. *Vremya Plameneyuschih derev'ev: Poeti Antil'skih Ostrovov.* [*The Time of Flamboyant Trees: The Poets of the Antillean Islands*]. Moscow: *Izdatel'stvo Vostochnoy Literaturi,* 1961.

Gayle, Addison. *The Black Poet at War.* Michigan: Broadside, 1972.

Gilroy, Paul. *The Black Atlantic: Modernity and Double Consciousness.* Cambridge: Harvard UP, 1993.

Goldweber, David. "Home at Last: The Pilgrimage of Claude McKay." *Commonweal* (1999): 11-13.

Hansell, William. "Jamaica in the Poems of Claude McKay." *Studies in Black Literature* 7 (1976): 6-9.

Hillyer Condit. "An Urge Toward Wholeness: Claude McKay and His Sonnets." *College Language Association Journal* 22 (1979): 350-364.

Hutchinson, George. The *Harlem Renaissance in Black and White.* Cambridge: Belknap Press of Harvard UP, 1995.

James, Winston. *A Fierce Hatred of Injustice: Claude McKay's Jamaica and His Poetry of Rebellion.* London and New York: Verso, 2000.

Janken, Kenneth. "African American and Francophone Black Intellectuals During the Harlem Renaissance." *The Historian* 60.3 (1998): 487-505.

Kent, George. "The Soulful Way of Claude McKay." *Black World* XX (1970): 37-51.

LeSeur, Geta J. "Claude McKay's Romanticism." *College Language Association Journal* 32.3 (1989): 296-308.

Lewis, Rupert. "Claude McKay's Political Views." *Jamaica Journal* 19.2 (1986): 39-45.

McKay, Claude. *Banjo.* New York: Harcourt, 1970.

—. *Complete Poems.* Urbana and Chicago: University of Illinois Press, 2004.

—. *The Dialect Poetry of Claude McKay.* Plainview, New York: Books for Libraries, 1972.

—. *Gingertown.* NewYork: Harper and Bros., 1932.

—. *A Long Way From Home.* San Diego, New York, London: Harcourt Brace Jovanovich, 1970.

—. *My Green Hills of Jamaica.* Ed. Mervyn Morris. Kingston: Heinemann Educational Book, 1979.

—. "A Negro Poet Writes." *Pearson's Magazine* XXXIX (1918): 275-276.

—. "Why I Became a Catholic." *Ebony* 1 (1946): 32.

Oakley, Leo. "Ideas of Patriotism and National Dignity." *The Routledge Reader in Caribbean Literature.* Ed. Allison Donnell and Sarah Lawson Welsh. London: Routledge, 1996. 91-93.

Said, Edward. "Reflections on Exile." *Granta* 13 (1984): 159-72.

Smith, Robert. "Claude McKay: An Essay in Criticism," *Phylon* 9.3 (1948): 272-73.

Vershinina, Z. "Introduction." *Banjo.* Moscow: Land and Factory Publishers, 1930.

Zverev, A. "*Poeti i Poeziya Ameriki.*" *Poeziya Soedinennih Shtatov Ameriki* [The Poetry of the United States of America]. Moscow: *Hudozhestvennaya Literatura,* 1982. 24-25.

STORIES THAT SAVE THEMSELVES: NOTES ON FIELDWORK IN ANGUILLA

DON E. WALICEK

Dey cut out my whole tongue
An' gimme half a tongue.
Dey hoodwink me from learning dem tongue
So I had to mek up my tongue.
Dis sweet tongue
Dat roll off it own proverbs.
Dis sweet tongue
Dat invent it own nungs and pronungs
An put words togedder
To make musical sentences.

Patricia J. Adams - "My Tongue"

As argued by James Clifford, ethnographic authority rests largely on two distinct tenets: the researcher's experience of "having been there" and the adjacent authority of "work," associated with empirical data, interpretation, and "science" ("Ethnographic Authority" 120). In this paper, I explore the relationship between these two types of authority, considering the role that memories and stories can play in the discursive construction of representations of the past in Anguilla, the most northerly of the Caribbean's Leeward Islands. In particular, I discuss aspects of linguistic fieldwork that I completed there in the summers of 2004 and 2005.[1] Finding a place for a set of personal stories and

---

[1] Fieldwork I completed in the summer of 2005 was funded by a grant from the Department of English at the University of Puerto Rico, Río Piedras. Other research I completed in Anguilla was made possible by the African Connections Project, a project directed by Dr. Nicholas Faraclas and Dr. Yolanda Rivera and funded by UPR's *Fondo Institucional para la Investigación* (FIPI). This essay was made possible due to the assistance and support of the Anguilla Library Service and Anguilla's Youth and Culture Department of the Ministry of Social Development. Special thanks to Ijahnya Christian, Jane Grell, Linda Lake, Russel Reid, and Jansie Webster. I appreciate comments on this paper received from the editors of this volume, Nicholas Faraclas, and Carol Moe.

recollections, I question and respond to assumptions and disciplinary practices which assume that the anecdotal, the so-called "subjective," is material of secondary importance to be trumped by "truth" and "objectivity." Clifford's approach to location as "a series of encounters and translations" rather than as a bounded space is one of the factors that motivates my shifting of attention from the analysis of synchronic phenomena to the relationship between processes of language and history-making ("Routes" 11). Accordingly, I call for an account of the past that refuses to relegate the "non-linguistic" and personal narratives to the margins, one that calls upon them to be centered, shared, and created anew in ways that simultaneously mirror and subvert similar processes of remembering and forgetting that exist among speakers of Anguillian and linguists alike. The final part of this essay juxtaposes a narrative from my experiences in the field with a discussion of Roy Harris's charge that historians seldom pause to consider the significance of philosophy of language.

Anecdotes have assisted me in better understanding different interpretations of one of the key terms that sociolinguists use in analyzing and imagining knowledge about language, the speech community. Dell Hymes sees the speech community as a primary concept that "postulates the unit of description as a social, rather than linguistic, entity" (47). He elaborates, ". . . sociolinguistics requires the contribution of social science in characterising the notions of community, and membership" (51). However, the criteria by which linguists group individuals in certain communities and restrict them from membership in others are not always as scientific and logical as standard linguistic practice assumes. William Labov expresses similar skepticism when he observes, " . . . it must be admitted that there is no agreement about how to define a speech community, and it may be asked whether the speech community exists as a definable object" (369).

Daunting questions about core concepts also linger in the study of Creole languages. Contemporary opinions seem increasingly to favor Salikoko Mufwene's assertion that "creolization" (the set of phenomena that led to the emergence of Caribbean varieties like Anguillian) refers neither to a particular kind of structural diachronic process nor to a "special kind of restructuring," but to "a social process" characterized by "... relatively greater [sociohistorical] ecology-prompted restructuring than in less heterogeneous and more focused settings of language transmission" (81). Mufwene's position can be related to Michel DeGraff's efforts to identify and deconstruct Creole Exceptionalism, the 'special treatment' that socialization practices and linguistic varieties in communities where Creole languages are spoken have received from linguists and non-linguists alike, treatment that in some ways positions Creole languages as inferior, emerging, simple, and/or otherwise different from 'normal' / 'regular' European languages. As the latter's arguments against exceptionalism show, the discourses that coalesce in a long-standing and somewhat uniquely situated approach to Creole languages are more tightly entangled with the consolidation of Western power and empire than has previously been admitted. Moreover, as DeGraff's copious analysis of linguists' and speakers' attitudes toward these languages demonstrates, myths promoting exceptionalism " . . . implicitly serve symbolisms of power and mechanisms of inclusion and exclusion, all of which relate to identity formation, to socioeconomic hierarchies, and to modern *missions civilisatrices* . . ." ("Linguists' Myth" 576). Unfortunately, a significant amount of research on Creoles still effectively rejects the very lines of inquiry in sociolinguistic theory and linguistic anthropology to which the research by Mufwene and DeGraff can be linked. Furthermore, according to one linguist's description of creolists' work in the field of sociolinguistics, "research in Creole studies is often restricted to rather narrow correlational variation," often employing ". . . models firmly rooted in the sociology of language of the 1960s" (Mühleisen 6-7).

***

Anguillian can be described as a Caribbean Creole language with roots in the nonstandard dialects of early English-speaking settlers of European descent and in the West African languages spoken by slaves and their ancestors. While Anguillian is seen as "broken" or "bad English" in some contexts, it falls into a category of languages that includes legitimate, rule-governed linguistic varieties that differ in systematic ways from recognized standard languages. Among these are other Creoles as well as minority and nonstandard dialects (Siegel 7). Anguillian is spoken primarily in Anguilla (also known as "The Rock"), an island which today is a British Dependent Territory. However, due to successive waves of out migration this community of speakers extends to places such as St. Martin, New Jersey, the Dominican Republic, and Britain. Presently this variety, which speakers may refer to as "dialect," "Anguillian," "Anguilla dialect," "Anguilla Talk," perhaps even as "English," co-exists alongside a "standard variety" of English that is recognized as the official language of the island.[2] Some linguists assume Anguillian to be an "intermediate variety" which has few "Creole features" when it is compared to more "radical" Creole languages (e.g., Jamaican, Sranan, Guyanese), despite the lack of written data describing this English-lexifier Creole and its sociohistory.[3]

---

[2] See Aceto for information on undocumented English-lexifier Eastern Caribbean Creoles. While the term "undocumented" is appropriate for describing Anguillian, see Banks and Christian for existing work on Anguillian.

[3] In this paper I define Creole languages using sociohistorical factors associated with British colonialism and the forced migration and enslavement of millions of Africans.

Anguillian's perceived proximity to varieties of English stems from Britain's expansion of its transatlantic empire to the Caribbean during the seventeenth century. According to most historical studies, Anguilla was first settled by the British in 1650 (Jones 12). While this year is significant in terms of Britain's establishment of this colony, early settlement was rather transient and other groups including the Arawak (sometimes referred to by scholars as Karifuna) lived on the island before this date. For example, in 1631 the Dutch succeeded in building a fort near the present-day village of Sandy Hill. Additions to the local milieu that arrived during the first hundred years of colonization include slaves of West African descent and indentured servants of European descent, as well as a diverse group of European settlers.

Anguillian's contemporary status as a "mixed variety" consisting of a unique configuration of substrate and superstrate features Creoles sheds light on the nature of interaction among the diverse constituents who comprised the island's early speech communities. The 2001 census estimates the island's population to be 11,430 (Government of Anguilla). The large majority of this population is of African ancestry. The first Africans probably arrived in the late seventeenth century, a time when most of the island's inhabitants were Europeans. But by 1717 there were almost twice as many blacks as whites in Anguilla. During the eighteenth century the slave population increased, due partially to the influx of persons of African descent from other British possessions in the region. In the nineteenth century, according to Barry Higman, the island received a high concentration of *bozales*, or African-born slaves, one of the highest among Britain's Caribbean colonies (123-124). Despite a strong African presence and the existence of plantations and harsh living conditions in the early period of colonization, myths suggesting that slavery in Anguilla "ended very early," "didn't really exist," or "wasn't that harsh" circulate within the island today (Petty 3).[4] While such beliefs sometimes beset the suggestion that the island's Creole maintains identifiable West African substrate features, they are complicated by archival evidence which indicates that abuse and exploitation associated with institutionalized racism and the Atlantic Slave Trade abound in Anguilla's past.

History not only offers up evidence of slavery, but confirms that racial hierarchy had a linguistic dimension. On some occasions slaves were brutally punished for ways of speaking. In one instance prior to emancipation, "the

---

See DeGraff for related discussions of anti-exceptionalist approaches to understanding the interface between Creole Studies, history, and ideology.

[4] Petty discusses beliefs that Anguilla was never a slave society and provides a detailed account of an incident in which six slaves were hanged at Crocus Bay in 1820. Slavery in Anguilla officially ended in 1838 when the St. Kitts legislature abolished the apprenticeship system provided by the Emancipation Act of 1833.

Court ordered the right hand of the mulatto girl Sally to be cut off for insolent speech to one of its officers" (Jones 18). While the details of this example remain to be uncovered, this event suggests that Sally, a slave of "mixed" (i.e., African and European) ancestry, was punished for the way in which she used language to critique the nature and effects of a socioeconomic system that treated her as property. Ironically, Anguillian and the sociolinguistic rules and norms shaping its use in the past and the present have emerged precisely for the same reasons that those who prosecuted her considered her critique of dominant power structures a violation of law and her dismemberment an extension of justice.

The violence associated with chattel slavery throughout the Americas did extend to Anguilla, even though the plantation economy never flourished there to the extent that it did on other islands. However, in other respects Anguilla's history qualifies as rather unique. For example, when positioned alongside statistics from other Caribbean colonies, demographic data from the nineteenth century point to three respects in which slavery on the island can be distinguished as somewhat atypical: proportions of children, life expectancy, and manumissions. First, as Higman explains, the largest proportions of enslaved youth were found in the "marginal colonies," smaller islands like Anguilla that did not produce large amounts of sugar for export (136). This had much to do with the fact that women of African ancestry were mothers to a large number of enslaved children. In 1827, for example, the island had one of the very highest slave child-woman ratios in the Caribbean (Higman 356). Second, slaves in Anguilla also tended to live long lives, despite harsh living conditions. In fact, it was one of only two British colonies in which the active labor force fell below seventy-five percent of the population (Higman 32). This difference was due largely to differences in age structure, as the island had a comparatively large group of older slaves and one of the longest life expectancies for slaves anywhere in the British Caribbean. Finally, a high rate of manumission characterized slavery on the island. Archival records from this period include accounts of slaves buying or otherwise obtaining their freedom and that of family members (Jones 17). It is the only island on which the number of manumissions in the three decades preceding abolition surpasses the number of slave deaths (Higman 379). Demographic data from Anguilla and other marginal colonies may be particularly relevant to sharpening anti-exceptionalist arguments which assert that creolization can be understood as a process of language acquisition and language shift. The historical phenomena that Higman draws attention to helps to demystify the notion that creolization differs qualitatively from those processes operative in similar situations involving non-Creole languages. Moreover, longevity within the speech community suggests the possible co-existence of and interaction among diverse lects across generations.

In addition to villages today comprised largely of persons of African and Afro-Caribbean ancestry, Anguilla maintains at least one "white enclave community," a geo-social space called Island Harbour that is said to be populated by a large percentage of speakers of predominately European ancestry (in this case, many are the descendants of Irish and Scottish migrants). In a linguistic study of this village, Jeffrey Williams makes a distinction between the vernacular variety used by some "clear" (a term which denotes white, light, or lighter skin) Island Harbour residents and the purportedly different one spoken by most black Anguillians (95). He claims that at least some speakers in this fishing village, namely a few elders living in an area called Webster Yard, speak a non-creolized dialect of English.

***

My interest in linguistic (especially Creole) Studies has led me to visit Anguilla five times during the last three years. On island I now work closely with employees of the Anguilla Library Services. During one of my early visits, I approached Linda Lake, the person in charge of the library's Anguilla Heritage Room, to discuss the possibility of collaborating to collect a diverse body of data on audio tape. I envisioned this fieldwork, a foundational component of my doctoral research, as what DeGraff describes as "Postcolonial Creolistics" and as what I proposed could be locally termed "linguistics as jollification."[5] Since then, we have aimed, with the help of many others, to create an archive of oral histories, interviews, and natural conversations that will be valuable not only for documenting Anguillian, but also useful for future researchers with interests in areas such as anthropology, history, folklore, and curriculum development. Early on in this research, my partners/collaborators at the library suggested that one way to get to know Anguilla and Anguillians better would be to participate in the Children's Library's Annual Summer Programme (CLASP) as an activity leader.

---

[5] In a 2003 discussion note DeGraff argues that "Postcolonial Creolistics" can improve the quality of life of Creole speakers in at least two ways: by producing knowledge about the history and structures of Creole languages, as well as their genealogy and sociology; and through the application of this knowledge to new and progressive paradigms in research, education reform, and language policy ("Against Exceptionalism" 44). Jollification is a traditional way that Anguillians come together and shared resources in order to accomplish a goal (e.g., harvest a crop, build a house, "chop ground").

I have completed two five-week stints on the island in this capacity. The first, in 2004, involved working with a group between the ages of ten to twelve that we called the Smugglers. With the theme "Book Dem," our activities centered on local stories and oral traditions (e.g., folklore, sayings, proverbs, poetry). The following year, my second CLASP experience was with the Riddim Rappers, young people from the same age range as the previous group. Guided by the theme "Let's Link Up," our activities centered specifically on communication.

Today a lack of information about the island's cultural heritage among many youth is one of the factors that often makes growing up in Anguilla drastically different from the experiences of previous generations (Simba 50). CLASP organizers consistently combated this problem in their interpretation of these day camp themes. But awareness that knowledge of Anguillian traditions (e.g., storytelling, serenading, string bands, performances by mocko jumbies and clowns) is seriously threatened prompts arguments that the island's culture needs more than documentation and reinforcement. As one CLASP organizer explains, "The time has come for us to rescue our cultural heritage, and preserve some of our customs and traditions. Yet there is need for more than rescuing – there is a need to rescue, rekindle, revive, and restore our cultural traditions" (Lake 2).

In addition to spending time with young people in CLASP, whenever I have had the chance I have traveled to different villages to record stories and conversations in Anguillian. Many of these recordings preserve the voices and stories of senior citizens, a group that some in the community have come to see and refer to as "culture-bearers." Because these elders are often well over seventy and possess knowledge of Anguilla's past and traditions that increasingly few others share, many locals consider recording members of this group "an urgent and important task." Nevertheless, because one of the project's aims is to eventually include recordings that attest to the internal diversity of linguistic forms within this speech community, we also organized sessions with young and middle-aged people. In recording culture-bearers, generally I accompany one of three Anguillians, each a facilitator and a speaker of Anguillian, on home visits that last from one to two hours. In many cases the facilitator, the person who leads the conversation, and the culture-bearer have been distant relatives, neighbors, or close family friends.

At first I considered the audio recordings the most tangible, important, and potentially insightful part of my research. While working with youth was rewarding from the very start, I felt considerable angst repeatedly trying to figure out how my time at CLASP would lead me to insight about the research project per se. It seemed that my involvement with the camp left me with little, if any, of the time and energy necessary to get a grasp of all the linguistic exchanges and sociolinguistic phenomena I witnessed.   With recordings I had data, language I could go back to, right there in my hands.   During this stage of my work I appreciated that they were something audible and concrete that I could later study.   Perhaps this is one of the reasons that I only occasionally sat down at night to type up field notes about each day's activities.   And when I did write, I tried to flesh out context: I described the places I went to record, the front porches I sat on, the clothes people wore, the goats that on one or two occasions interrupted us, background noises like roosters crowing and people cooking, the questions people asked me.   This was often done with the hope of going back later to fill in details, compose long lists of intelligent questions, and as someone might say in Anguilla, work out "tings not fittin togedda."

Since then I have gone back to cultivate this dry ground.   Looking back at my earliest scribblings, I assess the weight and significance of each idea and metaphor, phrases quoted verbatim from conversation, worries, thoughts that once qualified as breakthroughs.   Some new understandings have emerged over time: first, my understanding of what a speech community is suggests that members who contribute to its heterogeneity should not be overlooked; and second that, speakers express widely divergent, but not necessarily contradictory, views of Anguillian's relationship to Standard English.   These and related insights make once difficult questions seem less perplexing and the still puzzling ones more difficult to push aside.   Pouring over my notes, my tendency is to clean things up, to pull out useful empirical data, to gravitate toward conclusions, to move on, but sometimes I stop to look back.

I scan my notes for "culture," hints of where language and culture intersect, attempting to excavate patterns and order in "the messy stuff."   I notice my early attention to textbook notions of "data," metalinguistic commentary, and ethnographic observation: lexical items that might be unique to the island (e.g., *struck* "greedy," *ti* "it," *bank-up* "overcast," *aya*, an idiomatic expression perhaps particularly emblematic of Anguillian speech); young students telling me of being punished "for not speaking proper" when it was expected; a phenotypically white woman's explanation of how she can be "*clear*, but in a sense also black;" speakers who might pass for being native New Yorkers in one instance switching to Anguillian in the next; and my then mixed feelings about comments to a journalist that the library's summer camp would "help kids improve their English."   In my mind, each of these items always remains shrouded in a set of memories that is something more, a discovery, a situation, an explanation, an anomaly, an occasional confession.   The more time I spend thinking about language in Anguilla, the more I am pushed to value the stories that give continuity to looking back, the experiences that transformed a few daunting questions into some answers and a new set of questions, particularly the role the anecdotal can play in shaping understandings of the semiotic processes by which Anguillian and the social identities of its speakers are constructed (Gal and Irvine 79).

Looking back on memories allows answers to remain embedded in some of the processes that reveal their wake, in this case retaining and distorting their attachment to the experience of ethnography. Answers in this light may be better thought of as replies that reclaim a space for blanks inside answers than as conclusions that have been uprooted in order to "fill in the blanks." It is along these lines that remaining questions can be spoken of as being partially constitutive of other larger, relevant texts. Both shape the ethnographic encounter so that an outsider's coming and going to and from The Valley, the island's center, unfolds within a series of interrelated narratives and memories that is empirically supported yet also situated.

At the center of one set of these findings is "The Story of Wadu, My Great Grandfather," a story that was first shared with me and others in 2002, then transformed approximately two years later after I transcribed it in the process of looking back:[6]

This is a story that was told to me by my aunt, the sister of my grandfadda. She lived in Sain Martin. I stayed with her when I was small. My aunt told me dat Wadu and his brothers were taken to Dominica from Africa. There were four brothers: Kalil, Alewan, Abenji, and Wadu, the youngest. Somehow Wadu and he brodders got hold of sometin very special, a goat skin. Dey use it to mek a kettle drum. Wadu, my great grandfather, was just 14 years old or so. Dey made da drum and gathered with other Africans.

Wi da other Africans there, Wadu and his brothers held a special ceremony. They drew a big boat on da wall while the rituals was going on. There was da bangin of da drum, da dancin, and ting. And dey tol Wadu not to leave the room. But dey take *so* long dat Wadu get tirsty and he wanted a drink of water. While he was drinking da water, he hear da drums choppin and evertin, but when he rushed back in da room there was nobody in da room: ...everybody gan, ...boat and all, off the wall. And dey was never seen since, his brodders and all di Africans.

Wadu go on to become a man after, he got married and he had a wife now. One day da wife came crying tell him dat Massa tell her to bathe and get in bed til he come. At dis time he wife already have a baby for Wadu. And Wadu got mad and went at Massa wid he cutlas to cut em up. Den up come massa he had

---

[6] The video in which this story is told belongs to the Anguilla Library Service's Heritage Room. It was extracted from a discussion in which Mr. Connor, Dr. Joan Fayer, Dr. María Soledad Rodríguez, and Ms. Linda Lake participated. I assisted Sonia Fritz in recording the story and I transcribed it. Linda Lake, A-dZiko Simba, and I worked with the transcription for use in CLASP 2005. With help from the Tongue Clappers and Technochats, the Riddim Rappers dramatized the story for parents and other community members on the last day of CLASP 2005.

get da other slaves wid him. Dey surround him, tie him round, and dey beat him. Massa still very angry, so he sell him and he little son to a man from Anguilla. He wife stayed Dominica, but Wadu and he son go Anguilla by sea.

Years pon years after, slavery abolished but Anguilla ain't know it. You see, the government ended slavery but no one told di Anguilla people for many years. Dey didn't find it out until the 1840s or 1850s! When dey heard da news, da slaves set off for Sandy Ground to celebrate. Wadu, still working for di same man dat bring him from Dominica, decide he goin to da celebration.

Massa heard it. They were near a big garden he had in da area and he said, "How is it you're going to celebrate? Who gonna take care of my place?" Wadu answered, "It going to take good care of itself." After Wadu go to Sandy Ground, Massa decided to go in a part of de Garden dat Wadu kept for himself. He went in and filled he basket wi big, luscious fruit. When he came to leave he was going to get out and on one side up come a wall, he turned and another wall. A third wall came up too! An when he turned in the only remaining direction, what he see? Another wall! Massa crying out and dey tell his wife bout it. She come down, set out for the garden, and it turn out she can't get out either. Di people see he went in and couldn't get out so ain't nobody else goin in. People who see dis dey go down to Sandy Ground to tell him wha happen. Wadu say, "I didn't send nobody in der. Whoever in der, dey on dey own." And di massa and he wife dey were left dere.

Wadu didn't return until late and when he get home he sleep and dream bout freedom. Da next morning Wadu went down to di garden. He hold each one by di han, lead dem to di gate, and give em a kick. And ya know in doze days it was wrong to kick massa. Soon dey whip Wadu, but he was now free so he decide leave dem.

He start to pick up di few tings he had, among dem a horse dat he tended to when it was left to die. He call it Baby. When Wadu ready to leave, the massa tell em—"You can't take Baby, he's my horse. But, I tell you what, I got an idea: Let's make a bet. Let Baby race my horse Landash. You win, you can take whatever you claim, but I win and you work for me for twenty more years."

Wadu agreed. Dey decide the course of the race and Wadu put his oldest son up on Baby. Da race was a close one. Dey had to go around a big piece of land three times. Landash stayed in fron di first time round, di second time around. But di third time around, Baby pull ahead to win di race. Wadu took Baby wid him and he laid claim to a big piece of land. Massa say fine and gave him. But Wadu didn't go far, cause the land he won in da race sit right dere across from da massa's piece where dey been racin.

Today many people know da name of da two hills in dat area, one named for Wadu and one for the massa. But just a few know the full story that takes Wadu from Africa as a young boy and follows him to Anguilla where he got freedom and land of his own. (Connor 2)

Was this one of many Africa stories? What was the connection between the boy up on Landash and the belief that certain African *orishas* ride horseback? Was Wadu bilingual, multilingual? Did he speak an African language? Was it passed down to the teller in Standard English, Anguillian, both? Did his aunt use serial verbs and sometimes delete the copula? What was the exact context in which it was learned? How did he feel when hearing it as a child? Is the way he speaks "different enough" not to be "English?" Did the teller think this story should be written down? Would he have offered the story in a deeper, more basilectal form of Anguillian if all the listeners had been locals?

When writing now I sometimes find myself dwelling in the gaps revealed by interrogatives such as these, somehow caught up in the tension between "getting data" and "interpreting" my experience. When I first heard this story I wondered if it was somehow less valuable to linguists due to the fact that the narrative had so many features of Standard English. I had few questions about it and I saw one of my main tasks as the extraction of data from it. But now as I engage looking back, questions abound.

Initially I saw the task of preparing the Story of Wadu for the summer program simply as a way of "giving back to the community," as a timely opportunity to "put information back into the (social) system." It contrasted with "afternoon work," which entailed trying to "set up speakers" and "gettin deep, raw, real, basilectal Anguillian" for the subsequent study of language form and structure. Notes on the many steps and decisions it took to transform spoken memories of Wadu into dramatic production are absent from my fieldnotes. But I do remember a conversation with a young girl who had one of the most important parts in the play, the narrator. Though she usually came across as very articulate, she had noticeable difficulty reading her lines during rehearsals. In a private conversation with me she explained that she was from another island and had spent several years in the States. She asked for her part in "correct English," explaining that though she respected it she could not "do dialect" because she was not "B. H." ("born here" [in Anguilla]) and had "strict parents." As I translated her part, I began to think about ways in which the play exposed me to some of the phenomena that interest me most as a sociolinguist. I recalled a statement by Richard Bauman and Charles Briggs that evokes performance within as well as outside the culture it characterizes. As they remark, ". . . performances are often overtly concerned with deconstructing dominant ideologies and expressive forms" (66).

Passed down orally for generations, embedded in the tale of Wadu and the multiple contexts in which it has been represented are interstices that teach me how to listen not just more consistently, but in a way that urges me to make sense of and write about memory and other things a bit differently. In this light the story becomes relevant not simply for the light it sheds on the past and "authentic" speech, but for the ways in which it became implicated in the present. The task of narrating the play pushed the girl to recognize and discuss the impact of migration and family had on her own language attitudes. While her metalinguistic commentary shows insight and provides me with valuable data, perhaps more noteworthy is what happened in the final presentation of the play: she re-inserted a number of non-standard vernacular features into her interpretation of the script, making it clear that the prospect of performance had pushed her not only to share, but also to rethink her own attitudes toward Anguillian. As Bauman and Briggs hold, one option is to see performance as a process of enculturation, poetic patterning that "extracts discourse from particular speech events and explores its relationship to a diversity of social settings" (61).[7]

With the comments of Bauman and Briggs in mind, I turn back the pages of my journal to July 26, 2004 and I read and remember an incident from a day on which I wanted desperately to record people speaking but could not find anyone:

> It's not so easy, finding people to record. Today I walked around looking. I tried to find two people just kind of hanging out, "limin" as they say here. It wasn't so easy. [...] Saw a guy I thought was homeless on the way, the first and only one that I have ever seen in Anguilla. [...] He asked me for some coins. I gestured back a "no."

I fastforward about thirty minutes to an actual conversation with "the homeless guy." "Hey...how you doin? You from Anguilla?" He told me he was from Canada at first and that he had lived there for a few years. His English was very standard and he was extremely articulate, more so than I had expected. He said that he had gone abroad and that now was continuing to study "on his own." I asked where he lived before going to Canada. He said that it was Anguilla, his birthplace, and mentioned that he had been back for fourteen years. I was relieved – even though his specifics weren't exactly ideal, he *was* a possible candidate. I gave him a brief introduction to what I was doing and then just came out and asked him what I wanted to know:

Me: You speak the local dialect?
Him: English, We just got one language here. It's English. The only other languages are Spanish and some people speak French.
Me: What about the *local* English?
Him: It's English, like we are speaking now. You're a student, read the history!
Me: Oh, I mean the non-standard variety. You know, the way you speak when you are very relaxed or with close friends.
Him: It's all the same.
Me: What about Anguillian? Anguilla Talk? Dialect? Don't you think there's a difference...some sort of local talk, and then a standard variety too?

---

[7] See Bakhtin for a compatible view of how data situated as narrative can be oriented toward " . . . a world of autonomous subjects, not objects" (7).

Him: (slightly frustrated) No.
Me: (worried that he's annoyed) Okay, well just curious. You see some people
say there's another way here that is a little different from the way we are
speaking.
Him: No, dem don know.
Me: What about a way of speaking that makes teachers angry?
Him: That's shouting!
Me: (wondering if perhaps he isn't fluent in Anguillian, if he's internalized the
idea that Anguillian isn't worthy of being named, if he wants to hide something
from me): Can you understand everybody here in Anguilla when they talk to
you?
Him: Not the Spaniards and the French.

Okay, I was losing hope quickly. Picture me standing there dreaming of a
dissertation based on archival research. An elderly couple pass to my left and I
mumble "hello." The guy I was talking to shifts gears and mutters something
like–"mi lay-dee uuh gimmi sumtin naw pleeez." "Ay ain ga nuttin to giiv," she
replied, stressing the final syllable and raising the pitch at the end of her
sentence.

He sounded so different talking to her: his pronunciation, his intonation, his
choice of words. We chatted maybe a minute more. He had definitely grown
less interested in our conversation and the growing distance between us
suggested that he thought I was a little odd. Soon he said he had to go find
some money. We shook hands and parted. Then I turned back, "Hey,
everyting's cool, but just one ting, didn't you speak different with her, when you
ask for some money?" He looked at me straight in the eye, differently than
before and said, "Bai, yu a little crazy? Dat wha my question be."

For me ethnography has come to be largely about this and other stories that
narrate the processes of looking back and crossing, ones I share not only in this
essay and at home, but also with my friends, acquaintances, and new contacts on
"the Rock," in daily conversation, in discussing language attitudes, in recording.
Recollections such as the one cut from a journal entry and shared above give me
a story to tell, an Anguillian tale of sorts in which I am a character. I arrive as a
different sort of tourist-looking person, one who walks places rather than rents
from Avis, who speaks to guys who don't wear shoes and walk around asking
for change.

I reach and explore Anguilla with assumptions about "things" I have learned
to call and imagine as Creoles. My character carries a 600-dollar recorder and
Radio Shack microphones on his back, buys corn soup on weekends under Ms.
Mabel's tarp, and wants to get sixth formers interested in linguistics. He's
privately proud when the voices of Smugglers and Riddim Rappers scream out
"Teacher Don" from passing cars. Once he repeatedly pressed an eighty-seven-
year-old woman to tell him if Anguillians spoke "dialect" or "English," and

responded in disappointed silence, almost wounded, when she emphatically screamed back, "WE IS ENGLISH SPEAKING PEOPLE, DAT WHO WE BE . . . YES, IT'S ENGLISH LIKE IN ENGLAND." Now he desires more than just to listen politely and operate the recorder as others chat. More than two years into the project, increasingly he feels like jumping in to discuss cultural crossings such as this one.

When stories like those shared above become the topic of chat, certain elements are forgotten entirely while the importance of other details is exaggerated and seen as highly significant, ripe for commentary to be attached. "Being there" while also anticipating "being on the page" challenges me to engage at a more profound and personal level with people I encounter and the challenges of retelling. According to linguist Marianne Mithun, "If speakers are allowed to speak for themselves, creating a record of spontaneous speech in natural communicative settings, we have a better chance of providing the kind of record that will be useful to future generations" ("Who Shapes the Record" 53). There's a lot to be said about a recurring scenario in which the representation of Anguillian is shaped by speakers who intervene in ethnography as a storied event. In the aftermath of fieldwork, narratives direct attention to how things are retold and how to retell. They highlight nested and intertextually connoted ideas (e.g., talk of differentiation, migration, survival, conflict, celebration, communication).

Sharing my questions with Anguillians, I have come to replay voices as one way of allowing something engaging and useful to sprout. In the case of Wadu: "See, slavery in Anguilla was different, the slaves got land because sugar couldn't grow." "But, that isn't true, that part about the slaves not knowing about emancipation."[8] In the words of a mother, "You don't need to tell the story in dialect." "You know, I'm glad that you did it [the play] that way [in Anguillian], everyone here speaks proper English." It is this occasional clash of cultures that sustains my desire to look back. It makes a space for Wadu to be remembered as a speaker of an Afro-European language; for a linguist to be simultaneously a teacher, a tourist, a historian, and to come across as a little crazy; and, as suggested below, for all-ah-we to be English-speaking people.

The tale of my encounter with the "homeless man" ranks as incomplete until it grows to incorporate a sequence of unanswered questions: "What, a homeless person *in Anguilla?*" "Wha his name be? He ain homeless, you see he got somewhere to go, to sleep but maybe he has some problem." "Why you so worry about what language he talkin? Just conversate." "Maybe he trying to fool ya?" Following the effects of these reactions demonstrates that the

---

[8] Slavery in Anguilla began in the seventeenth century and ended in 1838. See Goveia and Craton.

boundary between "objective" and "subjective" ceases to exist when shared cultural forms mediated by language, such as local ways of talking, remembering, and putting things together, intervene.[9] The most colorful character in this story becomes a return migrant that I mistook for a homeless person who had internalized negative attitudes toward his native Anguillian.

Recounting conversations about the borders of community has also shown me that inferences about the borders of Anguilla's speech community should not be based exclusively on differences observed to exist within or between linguistic varieties (e.g., divergent rule systems, distinct registers, bilingualism), nor on the labels with which speakers refer to them. While naming is indeed significant for appreciating the tangled roots of Caribbean language histories, the speech communities in which varieties like Anguillian are spoken seem to be shaped largely by the extent to which ways of speaking that a linguist may see as divergent are linked by sociohistorical and ideological factors (Winford 97-98). Within this context, localized understandings and norms lead some speakers to see their language as a monolithic system (i.e., "English"). As Clifford writes, "Contact approaches presuppose not sociocultural wholes subsequently brought into relationship, but rather systems already constituted relationally, entering new relations through historical processes of displacement" ("Routes" 7). In theory, I knew that the community of Anguillian speakers was influenced by other communities (including immigrants, visitors, and, in local parlance, "nonbelongers" and the individual referred to as a "come here" or "C.H."). But as my bygone preference for "typical" and "genuine" speakers demonstrates, the tendency to disconnect entities by moving away from the boundaries of places and categories and toward presumed normativity is, as Penelope Eckert concludes, a strong one (108).

While offering this insight, I want to refrain from proposing that my looking back on experiences in Anguilla should attempt to eliminate problems at the center of debates about how to define Creole languages or a speech community. Ethnography, as I want to approach it here, does not strive to replace or reject purportedly flawed models vis-à-vis claims that it has discovered a more logical or systematic way of describing linguistic variation. Stories populating lived experience serve as a reminder that taxonomic systems, like representations of the past, are constituted in use. The questions about language and memory that they instill do not sit squarely with popular notions of history.

A related argument has been made regarding historians' appeal to notions of truth in their use of written language. Roy Harris rejects the positions of both autonomist historians and their postmodernist critics, claiming that history is

---

[9] See Volosinov for a discussion of how such dialogical research can contribute to deconstructing views of language and social life.

best defined by its own internal mechanisms, among which is language-making: "History is not a special case: all meaning-making, at all levels of communication in all societies, operates in the same way. History does not have a semantics of its own" (169). Endorsing an integrationist approach to understanding the past, he explains that the analysis of history-making should recognize at least three types of contributions: human participation in some activity worthy of remembrance, the work of historians, and the responses of onlookers, those who receive and interact with historians. Harris identifies these as *res gestae, historiae,* and *opinio,* respectively. His main complaint is that "with the exception of some [historians] who recognize the importance of 'oral history,' they make little attempt to research the formation of *opinio,* and thus leave a gaping hole in the fabric of historification" (174).

Like some culture-bearers who remind me that "history shouldn't always get in the way of a good story," Harris problematizes historians' decision to ascribe to language a degree of transparency that it can never achieve. Implicit to the stance he takes is the rejection of a surrogational philosophy of language, the treatment of words as surrogates of something else (e.g., languages, things, ideas, properties of "the real world"). From this critical perspective, history has the option of hearing the individual speaker-listener (whether ethnographer, culture-bearer, linguist, or "come here") as a historical actor entangled and mutually constituted by processes of being. Narratives built around ethnography remind science to investigate and revel heuristically in the meeting of epistemologies, in the questions that linger, and in the fear and inevitability of forgetting.

Works Cited

Aceto, Michael. "Going Back to the Beginning: Describing the (Nearly) Undocumented Anglophone Creoles of the Caribbean." Ed. Glenn Gilbert. *Pidgin and Creole Linguistics in the Twenty-first Century.* New York: Peter Lang, 2002. 93-118.

Adams, Patricia J. *A Gift of Fire, Cultural Writings to Enlighten and Amuse.* The Valley, Anguilla, 2003.

Bakhtin, Mikhail M. *Problems in Dostoevsky's Poetics.* Ed. and trans. Caryl Emerson. Minneapolis: U of Minnesota P, 1984.

Banks, Oluwakemi Linda. "Eh, Eh, It's the Language of Anguilla." *Tranquility Wrapped in Blue.* London: Hasib Publications, 2003. 33.

Bauman, Richard and Charles Briggs. "Poetics and Performance as Critical Perspectives on Language and Social Life." *Annual Review of Anthropology* 19 (1990): 59-88.

Christian, Ijahnya, ed. *Dictionary of Anguillian Language.* The Valley, Anguilla: Anguilla National Trust, 1993.

Clifford, James. "On Ethnographic Authority." *Representations* 1.2 (1983): 118-46.

—. *Routes, Travel and Translation in the Late Twentieth Century.* Cambridge: Harvard UP, 1997.

Connor, Michael. "Looking Back: The Story of Wadu, My Great Grandfather." Anguilla Heritage Room Oral History Project. *Library Lingo* 1.3 (2005): 2.

Craton, Michael. *Empire, Enslavement, and Freedom in the Caribbean.* Kingston: Ian Randle, 1997.

DeGraff, Michel. "Against Creole Exceptionalism." *Language* 79.2 (2003): 391-410.

—. "Linguists' Most Dangerous Myth: The Fallacy of Creole Exceptionalism Language in Society." *Language in Society* 34.4 (2005): 533-591.

Eckert, Penelope. "Variation and a Sense of Place." *Sociolinguistic Variation: Critical Reflections.* Ed. Carmen Fought. New York: Oxford UP, 2004.

Gal, Susan, and Judith Irvine. "Linguistic Ideology and Linguistic Differentiation." Ed. P. Kroskrity. *Regimes of Language; Ideologies, Politics, and Identities.* Santa Fe, NM: School of American Research Press, 2000.

Goveia, Elsa. "The West Indian Slave Laws of the Eighteenth Century." *Caribbean Slavery and the Atlantic World.* Ed. Verene Shepherd and Hilary Beckles. Kingston: Ian Randle, 2000.

Government of Anguilla. "Anguilla Census Data 2001." Updated May 2003. October 1, 2005 < http://www.gov.ai >.

Harris, Roy. *The Linguistics of History.* Edinburgh: Edinburgh UP, 2004.

Hymes, Dell. *Foundations of Sociolinguistics.* Philadelphia: U of Pennsylvania P, 1974.

Higman, Barry. *Slave Populations of the British Caribbean, 1807-1834.* Mona, Jamaica: The U of the West Indies P, 1995.

Jones, S.B. *Annals of Anguilla, 1650-1923.* Belfast: Christian Journals Limited, 1976.

Labov, William. "Is There a Creole Speech Community?" *Theoretical Orientations in Creole Studies.* Ed. Albert Valdman and Arnold Highfield 369-388. New York: Academic Press, 1980.

Lake, Linda. "The Oral Tradition and Our Development." *Anguilla Cultural Education Festival 2001.* Teachers' Resource Centre, The Valley. 22 February 2001.

Mithun, Marianne. "Who Shapes the Record: Speaker and Linguist." *Linguistic Fieldwork.* Ed. Paul Newman and Martha Ratliff. New York: Cambridge UP, 2001.

Mufwene, Salikoko. "Creolization is a Social, Not a Structural, Process." *Degrees of Restructuring in Creole Languages.* Ed. Ingrid Neumann-Holzschuh and Edgar W. Schneider. Philadelphia: John Benjamins, 2000. 65-84.

Mühleisen, Susanne. *Creole Discourse, Exploring Prestige Formation and Change Across Caribbean English-Lexicon Creoles.* Philadelphia: John Benjamins, 2002.

Petty, Colville. "Time Out." *The Anguillian* 13 August 2004: 3.

Siegel, Jeff. "Applied Creolistics in the Twenty-first Century." *Pidgin and Creole Linguistics in the Twenty-first Century.* Ed. Glenn Gilbert. New York: Peter Lang, 2002. 7-48.

Simba, A-dZiko. "Storytelling Preserves an Important Link." *Anguilla Life* XIV 1 (2001): 50.

Volosinov, Valentin N. *Marxism and the Philosophy of Language.* Trans. Ladislav Matejka and I.R. Titunik. Cambridge: Harvard UP, 1986.

Williams, Jeffrey. "The Establishment and Perpetuation of Anglophone White Communities in the Eastern Caribbean: the Case of Island Harbour, Anguilla." *Contact Englishes of the Eastern Caribbean.* Ed. Michael Aceto and Jeffrey Williams. Philadelphia: John Benjamins, 2003. 95-119.

Winford, Donald. "The Creole Continuum and the Notion of the Community as the Locus of Language." *International Journal of the Sociology of Language* 71 (1988): 91-105.

Part III

Narrating Women

PREPOSTEROUS WOMEN: THE TRUTH OF HISTORY AND THE TRUTH ABOUT WOMEN IN ANCIENT AND MEDIEVAL TROY NARRATIVES

NICK HAYDOCK

This essay explores the gendering of textual corruption in ancient and medieval narrative histories of the Trojan War. I will argue that both the rhetorical tradition and literary history gendered unauthorized supplements to the matter of Troy as grotesque corruptions of female forms, feminine bodies and the lives of ancient women. From the earliest narratives about Troy, through rhetorical and pseudo-historical traditions of ancient Rome and the Middle Ages, narrative discontinuities and adulterations are repeatedly figured as the monstrous feminine. These spectacles also index failures of self-control and creative power by male authors. Implicit in this process of gendering the *ordo* of literary works is the Aristotelian idea of matter (*materia*, here inherited legends and myths) that is given form by a masculine force. Hence failures of artistic control destabilize the dominance of form over matter, effeminizing male authors and serving to reveal their impotence. As poetic inspiration was also gendered feminine, it seems to have followed that poetic deceits, forgeries, and in-authoritative additions to traditional materials were also conceived as feminine. The internal (gendered) logic of historical supplements not only renders textual and narrative corruption feminine, but also repeatedly (and revealingly) takes the deceit and corruption of women as its matter. Put more simply, many of the lies told as the his-story of Troy unfolds across three millennia of Western culture are lies told about women, lies told about women telling lies, corruptions of textual and historical traditions which serve to corrupt women. I will argue that the gendering of supplements to narrative histories leads authors first to displace their failures and deceits unto onto their heroines and then to punish these heroines for imagined transgressions. In a sadomasochistic substitution authors, redactors, translators, and forgers fantasize moments of revenge or correction.

A final word on the organization of this essay is perhaps in order. I have not attempted to write a seamless, spotless essay on the discontinuities and corruptions of literary history. Instead I have tried to demonstrate the mutual implication of misogynist and rhetorical traditions across a broad span of time and texts through a structure that is itself digressive, asymmetrical, cyclic, and apposite—imitating exactly the lack of masculine control over my materials that the rhetorical tradition repeatedly warns against.

A Poetics of Artistic Failure

The *Ars Poetica* of Horace champions well-honed brevity over encyclopedic inclusiveness. One does not begin a poem on the Trojan War with Leda's quatro-zygotic egg. Horace further cautions the young Pisos against mountainous labors that bring forth only a ridiculous mouse. In reaching for the sublime, one tumbles into the bathetic, like the mad poet of the conclusion who in gazing at the stars tumbles into a well. But the bathetic and the grotesque are the satirist's stock and trade—a contradiction that allows Horace to write what is perhaps the supreme poem about bad poetry, all the most potent images of which satirize the foibles of poetasters. He continually returns to failures of continuity and incongruity, so that like Pope's *Dunciad* the *Ars Poetica* is less a recipe for good writing than an anatomy of contemporary artistic corruption and malaise. This anti-poem begins with an ekphrastic *satura*, a collage of ill-matched body parts whose totality expresses through its obscene contradictions the modern artist's failure of continuity.

> Humano capiti cervicem pictor equinam
> iugere si velit, et varias inducere plumas
> undique collatis membris, ut turpiter atrum
> desinat in piscem mulier formosa superne,
> spectatum admissi rissum teneatis amici?
> credite, Pisones, isti tabulae fore librum
> persimilem cuis, velut aegri somnia, vanae
> fingentur species, ut nec pes nec caput uni
> reddatur formae. (lines 1-9)

> Should an artist choose to attach a horse's neck to a human head, and paint everywhere various borrowed feathers onto a hodgepodge of pieces from every sort of creature, so that what began a beautiful woman ends in an ugly, rotten fish, my friends, granted admission to this risible spectacle, could you hold back your laughter? Trust me, dear Pisos, such paintings illustrate the book of a writer, whose vain fantasies are put together like a feverish man's dreams, so that neither foot nor head belong to the body. (translation mine)

The image became a *locus classicus* in the "Sister Arts" tradition that has alternately galvanized and bedeviled aestheticians since the beginnings of neo-classicism—on which see the inspired work over the last twenty years of W. J.

T. Mitchell (1986, 1994, 2006). What is of greater interest for our immediate purposes however is the meta-ekphrastic nature of Horace's portrait. He describes a virtual picture (note the subjunctive mood of the verbs) called here a *tabula*—a word in classical Latin usually associated with transcription and record keeping—and so thoroughly in keeping with what Mitchell notes are the promiscuous and semi-permeable boundaries of the "imagetext." But Horace's own imagetext is stationed at even one further remove: it is a poem about a painting that (perhaps unwittingly) illustrates another poem. Note too that what the reputed picture illustrates is not an image or a scene from the putative poem but rather its narrative structure (or lack of one). This is in complete agreement with the paradigms of the "Sister Arts" tradition as Lessing formalized them in *Laocoön*. Painting renders in space what poetry renders in time. Lessing elevates poetry in the *paragone*, whereas Leonardo would give the prize to painting, but neither in taking up the question posed by Horace's famous formula, *ut picura poesis*, ever really took on the nested, self-referential nature of Horace's own example.

The painting of literary structures is perhaps not as widespread as it might be, though certainly attempts have been made to "illustrate" the poetics of James Joyce's *Ulysses* and *Finnegan's Wake*,[1] just as one might read some *ekphrases* such as the weaving of Ovid's Arachne in *The Metamorphoses* or the tapestry of carnage woven with men's entrails by the valkyries of *Njals Saga* as images of these texts' structure or poetics. However, Horace's imagetext is not only self-referential—imaging his own poem's pastiche of example, advice and error—it is also self-effacing. At the very moment when it would seem to depend upon the viability of representations across different media it is also undermining the ontological distinctions between media that allow their intercourse. Horace's poem about a painting about a poem begins to unravel as we recognize the hermetic interiority of the poem illustrated by the painting described by the poem. His verses describe no extant work, that is to say not even any poem imagined as extant, and the painting which is a supposed mimesis of the structure of the supposed poem is also virtual, a sense well-captured in D. A. Russell's translation: "Imagine a painter who wanted to combine..." (in Leitch 124). Indeed I would argue that the subjunctive mood of the whole pastiche of word and image represents not a poem or a picture of a poem but rather the confusion of elements within an imagination that prevents artistic creation: the picture, if you will, *of a poem not being written*.

---

[1] See for instance the work of Paul Joyce such as "The Wandering Rocks," an etching which composes a portrait of the author from collage and puzzle pieces which reflect the "eighteen short vignettes" of Joyce's chapter.

The portrait of the mad painter is mirrored at the end of the *Ars Poetica* by Horace's own word portrait of a mad poet who mutters snatches of verse and falls into a well. Horace argues against pulling the fool back up again because he insists that the mad poet's bathos is intentional, like that of Empedocles who threw himself into Mount Aetna. We are to remember, I think, the grandiose designs of the poet in the opening lines whose volcanic eruptions yielded only a tiny rodent. Empedocles and the mad poet are fanatics who wish to seem divine but whose impotence is revealed in their desperate leaps of despair into oblivion. The ring structure of the *Ars Poetica* suggests that these mice have only returned to the fiery or dank wombs of their own pretentious imaginations.

Of course we postmoderns find the discontinuity of pastiche more congenial than Horace apparently did. The contributions of René Magritte the Belgian surrealist to the *paragone* dare to make real the ancient poet's imagined painting. In 1943 he composed "The Forbidden Universe" which displays a seductive, naked woman reclining on a daybed whose torso trails off into the tail fin of a fish. She represents the whole universe that classical canons of beauty would foreclose—the lower half of her anatomy is physically forbidding as well, perhaps hinting at the ultimate sterility of such hybrid creations. Ten years later Magritte replied to his earlier painting with "Collective Invention" (1953) where the direction of the reclining "woman" is reversed, and so too her parts: the dead fish-head makes the anatomically accessible torso much less inviting. Indeed, here we move from the 'forbidding' allure of the earlier painting to the stultifying image of an acephalous, phallic female sexuality. The diptych taunts us not only with the mix-n-match interchangeability of the two figures but also with their irreconcilable natures.

In the terms of a more famous series by Magritte we might say equally of "Forbidden Universe" and "Collective Invention," 'This is not a picture.' Or in keeping with the theme's direct descent from the Horatian *ekphrasis* we could caption them, 'This is a painting of a failed poem.' Or we might choose with ample justification to insist: 'These are not women.' However apposite these figures of failed continuity though, one thing they share is a certain desperate mortality—both are fish out of water, whether mermaid or flounder, and we know what happens to a fish out of water.

I want to highlight the sadism inherent in collage as artistic failure that murders in failing to integrate. In "Forbidden Universe" the oyster-shaped settee in its pinks exposes its red-fleshed treasure to the viewer's gaze like a recumbent Venus. She has obviously been posed by the artist but seems to have fallen asleep, until we remember what happens to mermaids who are kept from the sea for too long. The obverse of this image in "Collective Invention" if read from left to right offers us a similar but more complex lesson, perhaps in masochism, if we imagine the shapely legs and torso have beached the wide-eyed fish. What the pictures share in their juxtaposition of the grotesque and the erotic is a certain mockery of the masterful male gaze. Put another way, sagging fishtails and empty-eyed fish heads figure a male impotence that limply subverts

Figure 1: René Magritte "Forbidden Universe" (1943)

Figure 2: René Magritte "Collective Invention" (1953)

the Pygmalion myth of representational mastery.[2] And these failures, be they seductive or abject, are failures of continuity, of imaginative control, of restraint. In Magritte's pictures, just as in Horace's poet, we are allowed a peek at the artist's inability to sustain or master composition of the female and its deadly realization in abject images of women.

The images of Horace and Magritte detail a poetics of failure that recalls the monster Scylla, as well as the numerous references in the rhetorical tradition to a middle way between high and low styles; good writing is steering a middle way between Scylla and Charybdis. Teachers of writing can certainly sympathize with the insistence on a beginning, middle, and end that belong to the same composition. But in particular I want to note that Horace's metaphors for failures of continuity and concision, *ut pictura poesis*, are invariably the monstrous feminine. Leda's cross-species rape by the Swan leaves her with "an egg" and her torturous labor brings forth an apocalypse, in Yeats' formulation: "the broken wall, the burning roof and tower/ And Agamemnon dead." Poets (in Horace always male, though figured as feminine) labor like volcanoes, only to spew forth a ridiculous mouse. And male inadequacy in sustaining composition is figured as a dead fish at the tail end of a beautiful woman, an image, as I have suggested, that figures both creative and sexual impotence. Such poems are siren-like, sinister depths lurk beneath the song of Troy that never ends, it just goes on and on, my friends. Indeed, the Siren Episode in the *Odyssey*, after the unities of time and place in the *Iliad*, would seem to open up the specter of a Borgesian loop, wherein we regress not to the brutal concision of Homer's earlier poem but to the seductive, fatal encyclopedic impotence of the Cyclic poets. The Sirens' Song is an image of narrative-onto-death, Homer stops not only the ears of Odysseus' crew, but of his audience as well, for to give the sirens a hearing threatens to make the waywardness of Odysseus' journey and of Homer's poem eternal. Homer, then, allegorizes the seductions of open narrative as another instance of the monstrous feminine: in the oft-repeated metaphor of the rhetorical tradition, it requires self-denial and self-control for the poet to bring his work safely to port. Throughout the western tradition, of course, poetic inspiration is allegorized as feminine. The inspiration of the Muses is etymologically just that: by breathing their divine afflatus into the mouths of poets, they convey a spiritual influence, and so (to rationalize the myth like Horace and Pope) dull or mad poets are those who inhale too little or too deeply

---

[2] This Pygmalion dialectic of artistic impotence is uncannily imagined in the film "Genesis" (d. Nacho Cerdá, 1998), where a sculptor's reproduction of the body of his wife, who was badly mutilated and killed in a car accident, gradually transforms into human flesh while the sculptor himself slowly turns to clay. I have Gerardo Muñiz Villalon to thank for this reference.

of the divine spirit. Small wonder then that inspiration unchecked by male self-control should be repeatedly figured as a female monster.

Forging Faithless Women from Homer to Henryson

The debasement of women in Troy narratives is repeatedly allied with failures of artistic control, incomplete revision, and especially with false, incongruous supplements. Authors (perhaps unconsciously) screen their own textual deceits through dubious punishments for duplicitous women. In Book II of Virgil's *Aeneid*, Aeneas narrates the history of Troy's final night to Dido. This book contains the poem's most vehemently misogynist passage, one whose authenticity continues to vex modern scholars, just as it did late antique and medieval commentators. These controversial twenty-two lines (*Aeneid* 2. 567-88) do not appear in any of the ancient MSS of Virgil. They first appear in the textual tradition in the augmented version of the Servian commentary known as *Servius Auctus* or *Servius Danielis*, after the Frenchman who published it in the late sixteenth century (See Camps 114). The passage has retained its ambivalent place in the *Aeneid* as the poem's most celebrated crux; it is always included but usually italicized or bracketed in scholarly editions, yet its spurious status is often left unmarked by modern translators, as in the following version by Allen Mandelbaum:

> And now that I (Aeneas) am left alone, I see
> the daughter of Tyndareos (Helen) clinging
> to Vesta's thresholds, crouching silently
> within a secret corner of the shrine;
> bright conflagrations give me light as I
> wander and let my eyes read everything.
> For she, in terror of the Trojans—set
> against her for the fall of Pergamus—
> and of the Danaans' vengeance and the anger
> of her abandoned husband; she the common
> Fury of Troy and of her homeland, she
> had hid herself; she crouched, a hated thing,
> beside the altars. In my mind a fire
> is burning: anger spurs me to avenge
> my falling land, to exact the debt of the crime.
> Is she to have it so; to leave unharmed,
> see Sparta and her home Mycenae, go
> a victor queen in triumph—to look on
> her house and husband, parents, children, trailing
> a train of Trojan girls and Phrygian slaves?
> Shall Troy have been destroyed by fire, Priam

been beaten by the blade, the Dardan shore
so often soaked with blood, to this end? No.
For though there is no memorable name
in punishing a woman and no gain
of honor in such a victory, yet I
shall have my praise for blotting out a thing
of evil, for punishing of one
who merits such penalties; and it will be
a joy to fill my soul with vengeful fire,
to satisfy the ashes of my people.
And carried off by my mad mind
I was blurting out these words... (p. 48, lines 762-792)

W. A. Camps thought the lines probably by Virgil, but marked for revision or deletion in the poet's working drafts, and perhaps excised by his literary executors Varius and Tucca, who edited the poem for publication, against the express last wishes of the poet himself that the whole work be destroyed (123-6). Later Goold (1970) made a strong case that the episode is a forgery, arguing that it likely represents a fourth century composition inserted to smooth out a particularly vexed transition at this point in Virgil's text as it exists in the most authoritative MSS. Whether the episode represents authentic Virgil, marked for excision or revision, or a forgery positioned to smooth over a rough patch, it succinctly demonstrates the ubiquitous parallels between textual and feminine corruption in the matter of Troy. Repeatedly in this tradition, the will to punish feminine deceit inspires acts of textual deception, as doubts about the veracity of Trojan history are displaced into misogynist paratexts that hunt down and punish unfaithful women. Indeed, the description of Helen's activities on Troy's final night in Book 6 depict her as anything but cowering and helpless; instead she was a seductive double agent, leading a Bacchic dance with a torch around the Trojan Horse as a signal to the Greeks to commence their attack, and then hiding her (third) husband's weapons, and opening her bedroom door to Menelaus and Ulysses so that they can mutilate the defenseless Deiphoebus (see 6. 494-547). The incongruent, well-nigh mutually exclusive nature of these two misogynistic scenes, whether they are both by Virgil or not, reflects the uncanny doubling of duplicitous women ubiquitous in Troy narratives. The *Aeneid's* portrait of Helen on Troy's final night depicts her in two different places at the same time—as both trembling victim and hard-hearted *femme fatale*—exactly the kind of discontinuous, contradictory "portrait" of a woman that Horace travesties in the *Ars Poetica*.

The episode in Book Two is also remarkable because unlike almost everything else in the *Aeneid* it has no Homeric source; it clearly descends from the never-ending song of the Cyclic poets. The scene loosely imitates the opening book of Homer's *Iliad* where Achilles is prevented from killing

Agamemnon by the quick-thinking intervention of Athena, who grabs him by the hair. But perhaps the closest surviving analogue to the vexed passage in the *Aeneid* exists in Quintus of Smyrna's *The Fall of Troy* written in Greek in the fourth century CE, that is around the time when the questionable verses first enter the textual tradition of the *Aeneid*. Quintus clearly relies on the post-Homeric Cyclic poets, but in his version of the episode (Book 13, lines 385-414), it is Helen's betrayed husband Menelaus, not Aeneas, who tracks her down, inspired by "the dread Goddess Justice." He is stopped from killing her only by the timely intervention of Aphrodite:

> Menelaus amid the inner chambers found
> At last his wife, there cowering from the wrath
> Of her bold-hearted lord. He glared at her,
> Hungering to kill her in his jealous rage.
> But lovely Aphrodite held him back, struck
> Out of his hand the sword, his onrush reined,
> Jealousy's dark cloud swept away, and stirred
> Love's sweet well-springs in his heart and eyes.
> Swept over him strange amazement: powerless all
> Was he to lift the sword against her neck,
> Seeing the splendor of her beauty....
>   All his great strength
> Was broken, as he looked upon his wife.
> And suddenly he had forgotten all—
> Yea, all her sins against her spousal-troth;
> For Aphrodite made all fade away,
> She who subdues all immortal hearts
> And mortal. Yet even so he lifted up
> From earth his sword, and made as he would rush
> Upon his wife—but other was his intent,
> Even as he sprang: he did but feign, to delude
> Achaean eyes. Then did his brother stay
> His fury, and spoke with pacifying words
> Fearing that all they had toiled for would be lost.
> (Trans. slightly modified, Way, p. 555, 13. 385-95, 399-408)

As psychological allegory, the intrusion of Aphrodite perhaps figures both sexual desire and compassion. In the *Iliad* Helen is the creature of Aphrodite; she tries to abandon Alexandros (Paris), only to have the goddess threaten a dire reversal:

> Aphrodite rounded on Helen in a fury:
> "Don't provoke me headstrong girl!
> Or in my immortal rage I may just toss you over,

hate you as I adore you now—with a vengeance.
I might make you the butt of hard, withering hate
from both sides at once. Trojans and Achaeans—
then your fate can tread you down to dust!"
(Trans. Fagels, p. 142, 3. 479-85)

Such a violent hatred, by both sides at once, is precisely what the episodes in
Aeneid II and *The Fall of Troy* XIII rehearse, but unchecked anger is tamed by
desire, just as Aphrodite tames Ares in the ubiquitous myth of their sexual union.
In the *Iliad*, Helen, her anger chastened by lust, trots dutifully back to the bed of
Paris. In *The Fall of Troy*, memory and desire conspire to stay Menelaus' hand,
though he still goes through the motions of attempting to kill Helen in a
despicable face-saving charade, staged for Agamemnon's benefit. However, the
homicidium interruptum in the *Aeneid* is performed by the same goddess acting
in a very different capacity; she is not so much protecting the life of a favored
pet, as she is the psyche and the future of her beloved son, Aeneas. Her appeal is
not an allegorization of Helen's sex-appeal, but rather she entreats Aeneas to
return to the family he has left behind in his furious search for revenge. Clearly
the *Aeneid* passage rationalizes the hero's loss and regaining of self-control
according to a very different form of love than that which drives behavior in the
Greek texts.

We must remember, of course, that the *iliupersis* in the *Aeneid* II is a
putative autobiography, which Aeneas himself narrates to Dido upon his arrival
at Carthage. In making Aeneas his mouthpiece, Virgil brackets the narration of
Aeneas' history, which takes up, where Homer's left off, after the death of
Hector. What is being offered here is an official Augustan history, a defense
against the charges of treason and cowardice that plagued the reputation of
Rome's founder both before and after Virgil. In having Aeneas narrate his own
past, Virgil has it both ways: we have the truth from the horse's mouth, as it
were, but in having only his word for it we are reminded that in other texts
Aeneas is a horse of a very different color. Laocoön famously said that he feared
Greeks bearing gifts. The scholarship of recent decades has taught us to be
especially attuned to the dangers of Romans writing history, especially under
imperial sponsorship. Aeneas' self-told story is his version of the Trojan Horse;
like that of other famous gift-bearing Greeks, it hides menace beneath a pious
exterior.

Just as Book II of the *Aeneid* is poised to counter charges of treason and
cowardice, so too is Book IV driven by the need to defend Aeneas against
charges of being a callous seducer. Aeneas' survival suggests that he's got some
explaining to do: he embodies the paradox of a live hero. The apparently
destitute refugee arrives safe in Dido's harbors without a wife (Creusa) whom
he left behind when he fled the burning city—though we have only his word for

it that his wife's ghost appeared to him and told him not to bother looking for her! His subsequent, supposedly unwilling abandonment of *infelix* Dido, like his restraint in not chopping Helen into small pieces is God-inspired, Mercury descends to whet his almost blunted purpose, and Aeneas goes off to fulfill his historical mission in founding Rome. In order for nationalistic epic to be the "tale of the tribe," in order for it to explain the present as the inevitable result of the past, it must compose the most exclusive of master-narratives: there is little room for the niceties of historical accuracy (See Quint, esp. 3-96).

Ovid's response to the monologism of Roman imperial epic deploys counter-memory; his *Heroides* retells history from the perspectives of the women left behind. Dido's epistle to Aeneas is a suicide note, in which she takes the hero to task, before impaling herself upon his sword. Virgil invented the tragedy of Dido to parallel Rome's conquests and difficulties in the east, including Anthony's tragic dalliance with Cleopatra, which had led ultimately (and for Virgil ineluctably) to Augustus' vaunted *imperium sine fine*. But careful readers of Roman history knew that Dido and Aeneas could never have met; they lived more than a hundred years apart. In her brilliant book on Dido's literary career, Marilyn Desmond takes Virgil's rewriting of history to task. In essence she sees his historical displacement of a woman who was not alive when Aeneas landed in Carthage as a cold-blooded deceit in furtherance of Virgil's and his patron's imperial project: "so that the female might become identified with the colonized other" (Desmond 31). We might add that the colonization of history tends to render the female other as monstrous: as Dido descends into madness and witchcraft, she contemplates, Medea-like, the mutilation of Aeneas' son Ascanius and is compared successively to the Sirens, the Bacchae, and even Polyphemus. Late antique and medieval readers knew of Dido's troubling historical past as a virtuous widow, clever leader, and heroic suicide—troubling that is from the *telos* of imperial narrative. Macrobius outlines the way in which Virgil's eloquence encourages a collective amnesia of the truth about Dido:

> The beauty of his storytelling has been so powerful that everyone, aware of Dido's chastity... nonetheless overlooks the fable and burying the knowledge of truth deep in their minds, they prefer to have proclaimed as true what the sweetness of his feigning has caused to enter their human hearts. (qtd. in Baswell 19)

Homer had been dubbed the "father of lies" as well as the father of poetry by his earliest critics, Plato among them. Medieval readers knew precious little about Homer's poems, but they knew he was reputed to be a liar. The absence of his work, then, was no bar to his influence. In line with this tradition, the earliest responses to Virgil defended him against or charged him with Homeric plagiarism—theft being the least sincere form of veneration. Partially as the result of this Virgil was painted with the same brush as Homer, like father, like son—the conclusion was that Virgil had imitated not only Homeric lines, epithets, formulas, scenes and structure but that he had imitated Homeric deceit as well.[3]

As Homer was lost to the Middle Ages, the forged "eye-witness" accounts of the Trojan War by Dares the Phrygian and Dictys the Cretan were to hold sway in Europe for the first millennium and a half of the Christian era. What probably began as school-exercises in writing epitomes of the *Iliad* became, via their preposterous paratexts, the medieval authorities for the truth about the Trojan War. These texts focus on battles and funerals, paying little attention to women or to matters of love. In the late twelfth century Benîot de St. Maure's *Roman de Troie* remedied this oversight by re-casting the Trojan conflict as an episodic romance. His 30,000 line poem, roughly equal to the combined length of the *Iliad* and the *Odyssey,* details with psychological complexity the love-affairs of all the major protagonists. Guido delle Colonne's thirteenth century *Historia Destructionis Troiae* is in the main an expurgated translation of Benoît's work from French into the more authoritative Latin. Guido claims to be writing truthful history based on authentic and ancient sources, but his work closely follows Benoît's—with the romantic bits sharply curtailed. What takes their place in Guido are the virulent anti-feminist tirades he sprinkles liberally throughout his narrative. Indeed, Guido's extra-diegetic and extra-canonical anti-feminism is the single most original contribution he makes in this derivative redaction of Benoît, which he repeatedly assures is rigorously faithful to the supposedly unassailable authority of Dares the Phrygian.[4] Again authorial deceit and the punishment of feminine duplicity are two sides of the same forged coin.

---

[3] See, for instance, Guido delle Colonne's coda in *Historia Destructionis Troiae*: "I considered, however, the failure of the great authors, Virgil, Ovid, and Homer, who were very deficient in describing the truth about the fall of Troy, although they composed their works in an exceedingly glorious style, whether they treated them according to the stories of the ancients or according to fables, and especially the highest of the poets, Virgil, whom nothing obscures" (trans. Meek 265). Guido in general praises Virgil as the greatest of classical poets but even he is sometimes under the spell of Homer who "turned the pure and simple truth of his story into deceiving paths, inventing many things which did not happen and altering those which did happen.... Even Virgil, in his work the *Aeneid*, although for the most part he related in the light of truth the deeds of the Trojans when he touched upon them, was nevertheless in some things unwilling to depart from the fictions of Homer" (trans. Meek 1-2).

[4] For Guido's enormous influence on medieval English writers, see C. David Benson *The History of Troy in Middle English Literature*.

When the young Boccaccio took up the story in Florence in the 1330s, he saw in the widow Criseyde's betrayal of Troilus a *figura* of his own tragic love for Maria d'Aquino. Boccaccio renames Troilus Filostrato (killed by love) and retells the Trojan matter as a figural autobiography—precisely reflecting his real-life love affair and its dissolution when Maria's family finally married her off to another, richer man. The scathing anti-feminism of Boccaccio's later work like the *Corbaccio* is here only partly dormant. In the 1380s Chaucer transforms Boccaccio's personalized narrative into a grand romance epic. He too feigns an ancient source for his epic poem, whom he dubs Lollius, and vests the work's authority in apparent fidelity to its (forged) antiquity. It should also be noted for our purposes that Chaucer severely curtails the misogyny inherent in his two major, modern sources, Boccaccio and Guido delle Colonne.

To sum up this admittedly schematic literary history: the progressive corruption in the Troy narratives of the reputation of Homer's Chryseis witnesses the transformation of a girl freed in the *Iliad* from sexual slavery into a merry widow, "slydying of courage" who sleeps in quick succession with a young Trojan prince and the jaded Greek king, Diomedes.[5] Homer's Chryseis is quite literally speechless in the *Iliad* and we are given every assurance that she is returned to her father a virgin. It is as though her father Chryses' betrayal of Troy (from whose name her own derives) is displaced in later Troy narratives onto his daughter. Later poets certainly visit the sins of the father unto his daughter, but their progressive corruption of Criseyde also indexes their corruption of the ancient histories of Troy.

I believe that Robert Henryson, the last writer to add significant details to the Troy story, also knowingly deploys the by then well-worn trope of forging faithless women. As the last significant contribution to the matter of a story that had been almost 3000 years in the making, his work provides a kind of ironic coda to the whole, but one that is faithful only in its invention of punishments for women. In fact, it is as a contribution to the history of Troy that *The Testament of Cresseid* is perhaps most remarkable.[6] The fifteenth century Scottish poet reaches back into the mists of tradition to torture and kill an unfaithful heroine—a temptation, as we have seen, that was present in Homer's earliest readers. In Chaucer's recension of the Troy narrative (like all those before him) Criseyde simply fades away after the alienation of her affections

---

[5] Throughout I have used the spellings of this woman's name as they appear in the texts under consideration, hence Chryseis, Briseida, Criseyde, Cresseid all refer to the same figure, though not perhaps to the same character, since each author presents her in distinctive ways.

[6] C. David Benson rightly notes that the *Testament* "contains not one scene from the historical tradition" (143), but underestimates, as I hope to show, Henryson's use of works in the historical tradition.

from Troilus to Diomede cause Troilus' death at the hands of the "fierce Achille." Henryson picks up the story not at the end of Chaucer's narrative but at the point in Book V when Criseyde disappears from the text. In situating itself within rather than after Chaucer's work, Henryson's poem is yet another preposterous paratext, which kills Cresseid but leaves Troilus alive to mourn her death. Her fall is rapid: Diomede, his appetite for her quickly reaching a disgusted satiety, abandons Cresseid, and she tumbles even further into promiscuity and finally prostitution:

> Quhen Diomeid had all his appetyte,
> And mair, fulfillit of this fair ladie,
> Vpon ane vther he set his haill delyte,
> And send to hir a lybell of repudie
> And hir excludit fra his companie.
> Than desolate scho walkit vp and doun,
> And sum men sayis, into the court, commoun. (lines 71-77)

Henryson is renowned as perhaps the greatest of the Chaucerians but this stanza especially reaches back to earlier texts in the matter of Troy for its devastating ironies, just as it grotesquely augments traditional portraits of Cresseid as "inconstant." Diomede's suffering like a courtly lover is much curtailed by Chaucer; there is no mention, as there is in Guido, that his desire inconveniences him at all. Guido though tells us that: "He had no appetite for food and drink" (Trans. Meek 164). Benoît has Diomede assure Criseyde: "So long will I beseech you till you have mercy on me. This I wait for; this I crave; this I long for; this I desire. Then my sighs will have an end. *All my joy will be fulfilled as soon as I possess you*" (Trans. Gordon 17, my emphasis). The innocent tropes of courtly love are pushed literally *ad nauseam* by Henryson, as Diomede reaches a state of disgusted satiety with Cresseid ("all his appetite/ and mair fulfillit..."). Shakespeare would engorge himself even further on the theme of sexual nausea in his contributions to the corruption of Cressida in his play, just as he would dub her "a daughter of the game"—ideas that derive directly or indirectly from Henryson. Indeed, the Scottish poet actualizes the anti-feminist response of his *auctores* to Cresseid's betrayal of Troilus, turning the bitter predictions of Troilus in the *Roman de Troie* that she will ultimately become a prostitute and Guido's comparison of her to whores into a fact of her biography, having her "go amang the Greikis air and lait,/ sa giglotlike takand thy foull plesance" (82-3). Henryson would seem to question his sources' portrayal of Cresseid as a prostitute ("sum men sayis") but of course they say nothing of the sort; they simply use her inconstancy as the occasion for anti-feminist tirades.[7]

---

[7] Benoît puts the harshest condemnations of Criseyde into the mouth of the spurned

The Scottish poet's augmentation of Cresseid's inconstancy produces a portrait every bit as grotesque as Horace's picture of the abject feminine which serves to image incongruous supplements to traditional historical matters. Verbal portraits of the main actors in the Trojan War descend from Dares. Chaucer withholds the verbal portraits of Troilus, Criseyde and Diomede until near the end of his poem. His portrait of Criseyde focuses on her physical beauty and courtly virtues, and only at the end does it refer briefly to her traditional "slydynge of corage" (5.806-826; 825).[8] Henryson deforms this traditional portrait significantly not only by darkening her moral character further than any previous source but also by defacing her famous beauty with leprous spots. In Homer Chryseis is a figure of exchange, a slave girl given back to her father Chryses in perhaps the earliest example of the patriarchy's "trade in women." In the medieval histories of Troy her father's deceitfulness as a traitor to Troy is extended to her, as her exchange for the prisoner Antenor becomes the occasion of the transfer of her affections from Troilus to Diomede. She thus becomes no longer simply a figure of exchange but of mutability, a figure of change itself. In Henryson her changeability becomes at last a physical metamorphosis as she is punished by the gods with leprosy.

Troilus who taunts her new lover Diomede with these words: "By you I send her word that we two are parted. If you have been to her what I used to be, there will be plenty more accepted lovers before the siege is ended; you will have to keep good watch. You may have her wholly to yourself now, but she has not yet made an end, since she finds pleasure in the trade of love. For, if there are so many that somewhat please her, the very innkeepers will have her favours. It will be wise for her to take thought from whom she may draw profit" (trans. Gordon 18-19). Guido cuts this speech entirely, noting only that "Troilus... taunted Diomedes with opprobrious words for loving Briseida (i.e., Criseyde). He prefers to comment himself on her inconstancy and to extend the principle of feminine deceit and mutability to all women, which he refuses to discuss in a damning *praeteritio*: "That day had not yet declined toward the hours of evening when Briseida has already changed her recent intentions and the former plan of her heart.... Already the love of the noble Troilus began to moderate in her heart, and in such a short time, so suddenly and unexpectedly, she became inconstant and began to change in everything. Accordingly, what is to be said about the constancy of women, whose sex has as its property to dissolve its plans with sudden frailty and to change and be fickle in the shortest time? For it does not fall to a man to be able to describe their fickleness and wiles, since their flighty intentions are more wicked than it is possible to say" (trans. Meek 160).

[8] Chaucer's portraits derive from those of Dares probably through the intermedium of Joseph of Exeter. But the final element, "slydyng of corage," is in neither source and hence represents another small instance of an inauthentic supplement to the portraits of the historical tradition.

I would compare Henryson's fatal transformations of Cresseid with the earlier episodes in Homer, Virgil, and Quintus Smyrnaeus discussed above, though here the vengeful punishment for a wayward woman hiding in a temple is actually carried out—rather than prevented—by the gods themselves. The court of planetary deities who preside over Cresseid's case suggest that her "crimes" against love have been augmented by her blasphemy against the gods of love, Cupid and Venus. Henryson's scene at least partially derives from an episode in the historical tradition. Guido has Briseida upon her return to her father berate him for his treason:

> Indeed you have been deceived by the trifling replies of Apollo, who you say, ordered you to desert your ancestral home and your gods in bitter hatred and to attach yourself thus closely to your enemies. Obviously it was not the god Apollo, but rather, I think, a band of infernal furies from whom you received such a reply. (Trans. Meek 159)

This is the shrillest we ever see Briseida in the historical tradition, indeed she comes close here to the blasphemy she finally commits in Henryson's version. Briseida's complaint emphasizes that her father has relied upon the lying prophecies of a god he supposes to be Apollo and in so doing has made himself infamous, poor and an exile—exactly the terms which she uses to berate the "replies" of her gods, Venus and Cupid, in Henryson's *Testament of Cresseid*:

> "Allace, that euer I maid 3ow sacrifice!
> 3e gaue me anis ane deuine responsaill
> That I suld be the flour of luif in Troy;
> Now am I maid ane vnworthie outwaill,
> And all in cair translatit is my ioy.
> Quha sall me gyde? Quha sall me now conuoy,
> Sen I fra Diomeid and nobill Troylus
> Am clene excludit, as abiect odious?" (lines 126-133)[9]

In Guido's *Historia* Briseida imagines that her father has been stigmatized by both Greeks and Trojans for his treason, an exile "defamed and blackened by the stigma of such a disgrace" (159), but in Henryson it is she who suffers exile (outwaill) and is excluded from the company of both her Greek and her Trojan lovers. Her blasphemy calls down upon her the vengeance of the gods as well, as she is "blackened" by the leprous pustules with which the gods afflict her. The parallel with Helen in narratives of Troy's destruction is palpable. She like Helen hides in a temple fearing the hatred of both sides at once. Note though

---

[9] In Henryson's version her father Calcas is made a priest of Venus, not of Apollo, perhaps to bring her blasphemy more in line with her other crimes against love.

that in Henryson's version Venus is no longer the wayward woman's protector but rather her scourge. Indeed the scene uncannily recalls Aphrodite's threat in the *Iliad* (which Henryson probably did not know) cited above. The gods afflict Cresseid with a venereal disease (leprosy was often confused in the late fifteenth century with syphilis and was thought to be transmitted through sexual intercourse) and her poetically just punishment includes the immediate destruction of her beauty, followed by the slow and painful death of her body.

Henryson's ending is invented out of whole cloth, there is no classical or even medieval authority for the illness and death of Cresseid. In turning the heroine leaden gray, in covering her with spots and in killing her off, Henryson offers a hideous coda to Chaucer's portrait of the beautiful, if mutable Criseyde. Both the discontinuities between the two texts as well as the rather grotesque tail Henryson affixes to Chaucer's work perhaps should remind us of Horace's attractive woman who ends as a dead fish. Yet rather than attempting to hide the work's incongruence, Henryson foregrounds it in his preface. He presents himself as reader of Chaucer's *Troilus and Criseyde* who "discovers" another book of spurious authority that contradicts the way Chaucer's work ends. Henryson's gesture is both transparent ruse and self-parody: it is his own book which he imagines already up there on the shelf beside the most revered work of Britain's most revered author. Henryson takes the unprecedented step for a Chaucerian of suggesting that not everything that Chaucer wrote was true, but in the same breath undermines the forged authority of his own text as well, admitting he does not know whether it is "authroeist or fenyit of the newe." The gesture seems to recognize the extent to which punishing women entails one's own credibility: in blackening the reputation of ancient women, authors sacrifice their personal integrity and the authority of their works. But that was a price the humanist in Henryson was more than willing to pay. His supplement to the history of Troy and the life of Cresseid is a grotesque coda. Despite its pathos and sublimity, and despite the tragic recognitions her tortures provoke in Cresseid herself, the tale (tail) remains abjectly grotesque. The poem is a testament to the uncanny conflations of sexual and textual corruptions that plague pre-modern histories of Troy.

Works Cited

Baswell, Christopher. *Virgil in Medieval England: Figuring the* Aeneid *from the Twelfth Century to Chaucer.* Cambridge: Cambridge UP, 1995.

Benoît de Sainte-Maure. *Le Roman de Troiae.* Ed. Léopold Constans. Société des Anciens Textes Français, 6 vols. Paris: Firmin Didot et Cie., 1904-12.

Benson, C. David. *The History of Troy in Middle English Literature: Guido delle Colonne's* Historia Destructionis Troiae *in Medieval England.* Woodbridge, Suffolk, UK: D. S. Brewer, 1980.

Camps, W. A. *Virgil's Aeneid.* Oxford: Oxford UP, 1969.

Chaucer. *The Riverside Chaucer.* 3rd. ed. Larry D. Benson, gen. ed. New York: Houghton Mifflin, 1987.

Da Vinci, Leonardo. "Paragone: Of Poetry and Painting." In *Treatise on Painting*, ed. A Phillip McMahon. Princeton: Princeton UP, 1956.

Dares. *Daretis Phrygii De Excidio Troiae Historia.* Ed. Ferdinand Meister. Leipzig: Teubner, 1873.

Dares and Dictys. *The Trojan War: The Chronicles of Dictys of Crete and Dares the Phrygian.* Bloomington: Indiana UP, 1966.

Dictys. *Dictis Cretensis Ephemeridos Belli Troiae Libri.* Ed. Werner Eisenhut. Leipzig: Teubner, 1958.

Desmond, Marilynn. *Reading Dido: Gender, Textuality, and the Medieval Aeneid.* Minneapolis: University of Minnesota Press, 1994.

Goold, G. P. "Servius and the Helen Episode." *Harvard Studies in Classical Philology* 74 (1970): 101-68.

Gordon, R. K. *The Story of Troilus as Told by Benoît de Sainte-Maure, Giovanni Boccaccio, Geoffrey Chaucer, Robert Henryson.* Medieval Academy Reprints for Teaching. Toronto: University of Toronto Press, 1978, 1995.

Guido delle Colonne. *Historia Destructionis Troiae.* Ed. Nathaniel Edward Griffin. Cambridge: The Medieval Academy of America, 1936.

—. *Historia Destructionis Troiae.* Trans. Mary Elizabeth Meek. Bloomington: Indiana UP, 1974.

Henryson. *The Poems of Robert Henryson.* Ed. Denton Fox. Oxford: Clarendon Press, 1981.

Homer. *Homer: The Iliad.* Trans. Robert Fagles. New York: Penguin Classics, 1990.

Horace. *Q. Horati Flacci: Opera.* Edward C. Wickham and H. W. Garrod Oxford: Clarendon Press, 1901, 1984.

Leitch, Vincent B., gen. ed. *The Norton Anthology of Theory and Criticism.* New York: Norton, 2001.

Lessing, Gotthold Ephraim. *Laocöon: An Essay upon the Limits of Painting and Poetry.* Trans. Ellen Frothingham. New York: Noonday Press, 1957.

Mitchell, W. J. T. *Iconology: Image, Text, Ideology.* Chicago: University of Chicago Press, 1986.

—. *Picture Theory.* Chicago: University of Chicago Press, 1994.

—. *What Do Pictures Want?* Chicago: University of Chicago Press, 2006.

Ovid. *Ovid: Heroides: Select Epistles.* Ed. Peter E. Knox. Cambridge: Cambridge UP, 1995, 61-67.

Quint, David. *Epic and Empire: Politics and Generic Form from Virgil to Milton.* Princeton: Princeton UP, 1993.

Smyrnaeus, Quintus. *Quintus Smyrnaeus: The Fall of Troy.* Trans. A. S. Way. Loeb Classical Library 19 (Cambridge, MA: Harvard UP, 1913, 2000).

Virgil. *The Aeneid of Virgil: A Verse Translation.* Trans. Allen Mandelbaum. New York: Bantam, 1971.

A VIOLENT HOMELAND: RECALLING HAITI IN EDWIDGE DANTICAT'S NOVELS

DORSÍA SMITH

As Kim Worthington has pointed out, "Despite the fallibility of memory and the partiality of our subjective interpretations, the narratives we tell about our world and ourselves anticipate coherence and closure or, at the very least, followability…. Narrative conceptualization enables the creation of a revisable, provisional, but more or less readable self, and facilitates the experience of self-continuity through time (15)." Edwidge Danticat's protagonists tell their stories by reconnecting with their Haitian heritage and by recalling their homeland as a beautiful though dangerous country in her novels *Breath, Eyes, Memory* and *The Dew Breaker*. This danger comes from widespread violence caused by the corrupt rule of Haiti's former President François "Papa Doc" Duvalier who won the presidency in 1957 and changed the constitution in 1964 to declare himself "president for life" (Hillman & D'Agostino 119). Upon his death in 1971, Jean-Claude "Baby Doc" Duvalier assumed his father's position as President. Both "Papa Doc" and "Baby Doc" used the threatening volunteer policemen known as the Tonton Macoutes. Their damaging legacy continued until "Baby Doc" *Current* was exiled to France in 1986. Even after the expulsion of the Tonton Macoutes and Duvalier, Haiti has continued to be beleaguered with political violence and instability. For example, the recent election of René Préval as President in February 2006 was considered a fraud by thousands of Haitians who took to the streets in aggressive protest. It seems that somehow Haiti is struggling to heal the wounds of its violent past as this legacy lingers and impedes Haiti's rehabilitative progress to eradicate social, political, and economical unrest. ✶

Breath, Eyes, Memory narrates the painful journey of Sophie Caco, a young Haitian woman who moves to New York. She is frequently haunted by her disturbing memories of Haiti's political violence and the cruel acts committed by the Tonton Macoutes. *The Dew Breaker* also recalls the history of the abusive Tonton Macoutes by blending their documented acts with unofficial tales of their domineering powers. Danticat reconstructs the Macoutes' violent reign by collecting the memories of those Haitian who suffered under their vindictive rule. In the novel, Mr. Bienanime is a former Tonton Macoute who has committed political assassinations and torture under Duvalier's rule. As in *Breath, Eyes, Memory*, Danticat accurately depicts the Tonton Macoutes as violent physical and mental torturers who inflict pain without mercy. She reveals how their violence is linked to Haiti's continued economic decline, turmoil, and political strife. This perspective is shared by scholars Michael Dash and Myriam J.A. Chancy who have documented Haiti's troubled histories, including its political and financial instability in their books *Haitian Quest for Freedom* (1999) and *Framing Silence: Revolutionary Novels by Haitian Women* (1997).

The narrator of *Breath, Eyes, Memory*, Sophie Caco, lives in the countryside in Haiti. While Sophie enjoys her caring and friendly neighbors, she must endure the harshness of living in a village which is stricken by poverty, brutality, and illiteracy. In particular, many of the villagers are uneducated and are forced to work in the rough cane fields to earn a meager living. In order for Sophie to acquire a solid education and be free from the violence and oppression entrenched in Haiti, her Tante Atie and her Grandmother Ife send her to her mother in New York. On her way to the airport, Sophie is reminded of the widespread strife in Haiti; she has to pass soldiers shooting down student demonstrators protesting against the government:

> Some of the students fell and rolled down the hill. They screamed at the soldiers that they were once again betraying the people. One girl rushed down the hill and grabbed one of the soldiers by the arm. He raised his pistol and pounded it on top of her head. She fell to the ground, her face covered with her own blood. (34)

As one character tells her, "There is always some trouble here [in Haiti]" (33). Furthermore, the Tonton Macoutes "roam the streets in broad daylight, parading their Uzi machine guns" (138). During one such incident, Sophie observes a Macoute strike a coal vendor for allegedly stepping on his foot. Even though the coal vendor lies helplessly in a fetal position and spits blood, additional Macoutes callously step on him with their boots. The surrounding citizens stand silently in shock and fear and Sophie is cautioned by her Grandmother to move on or face "liv[ing] [her] nightmares [of being attacked] too" (118).

Sophie's mother, Martine, also escapes from Haiti because of the threat of violence. After being raped by a member of the Tonton Macoutes, Martine fears "he [the rapist] would creep out of the night and kill her in her sleep" (139). To protect her, she is sent by her mother to live with another family. After giving birth to Sophie, Martine leaves the island and migrates to New York. While Tante Atie reminds Sophie that "in this country, there are many good reasons for mothers to abandon their children" (20), her fear is that her mother left because Sophie was a daily reminder of the danger of the Macoutes.

Her fears are substantiated when Martine tells her that she physically resembles her rapist father: "But now when I look at your face I think it is true what they say. A child out of wedlock always looks like its father" (61). With the troubling realization that she looks like "no one in [her] family" (45), Sophie becomes fixated with the identity of her father and her mother's rape:

> My father might have been a Macoute. He was a stranger who, when my mother was sixteen years old, grabbed her on the way back from school. He dragged her into the cane fields, pinned her down on the ground. He had a black bandanna over his face so she never saw anything but his hair, which was the color of eggplants. He kept pounding her until she was too stunned to make a sound. When he was done, he made her keep her face in the dirt, threatening to shoot her if she looked up. (139)

She hopes that she has only inherited her father's physical composition and not his violent characteristics. In order to repel any violent emotions, Sophie becomes the opposite and is frequently passive when she interacts with her mother by not voicing any opposition to her.

As a result of being raped, Martine envisions "the rapist everywhere" (199) and suffers from nightmares which Sophie often witnesses. She says, "I would hear her [Martine] screaming for someone to leave her alone. I would run over and shake her as she thrashed about" (81). Sophie also suffers from nightmares and worries if they are "hereditary or [. . .] something [. . .] caught from living with her [mother]" (193). Martine and Sophie's nightmares both represent distorted images of Martine's rapist–dreams "about the same thing: a man with no face, pounding a life into a helpless young girl" (193). They undergo this mental anguish because of the oppressive treatment of women by the Tonton Macoutes:

> When they [the Macoutes] entered a house, they asked to be fed, demanded the woman of the house, and forced her into her own bedroom. Then all you heard was screams until it was her daughter's turn. If a mother refused, they would make her sleep with her son and brother or even her own father. (139)

According to Donette A. Francis in her essay "'Silences Too Horrific to Disturb': Writing Sexual Histories in Edwidge Danticat's *Breath, Eyes, Memory*," the Tonton Macoutes used rape as a "notorious method of maintaining their power" and wielding terror among Haitians (80). Rape survivors feared further retaliation from the Tonton Macoutes while the remaining targets worried about their potential subjection to sexual violations. Hence, the unreported sexual assaults remain "invisible" and Duvalier's regime uses these unspoken narratives to quell any future narratives of rape and sexual misconduct by the Tonton Macoutes.

Sophie later recognizes that her mother's unpunished rape bears a similiarity to the power of the Tonton Macoutes in children's stories: "the Tonton Macoute was a *bogeyman*, a scarecrow with human flesh. He wore denim overalls and [. . .] always had scraps of naughty children, whom he dismembered to eat as snacks" (Danticat 138). Children hide from the mythological bogeyman because they are told, "If you don't respect your elders, then the Tonton Macoute will take you away" (138). Like the children in the fairy tales, women flee when they see the dangerous Tonton Macoutes. They know that the Macoutes sexually abuse women and then use their authority to keep these acts "hidden." Furthermore, they utilize their control to intimidate women into leaving Haiti. The end result is a government which refuses to address the sexual violence committed against women and dismisses women's tales of mistreatment as unreal. In her essay "Challenging Violence: Haitian Women Unite Women's Rights and Human Rights," Anne Fuller also blames the Tonton Macoutes' acts of violence on the lack of rights and protections women have under Haitian law. In particular, she points out that rape is not defined in the law and that women need medical certificates to prove rape (41). With laws that discourage and encumber the reporting of rape, women are again subjected to a framework that supports their cruel and unequal treatment. As such, Sophie and her mother's traumas parallel Haiti's traumatic experiences and in particular, the people's recollections of violence, oppression, suffering, and fear.

Martine's inability to convey her experience of sexual violence leads to more psychological trauma than nightmares. Because Haitian culture dictates that a raped woman loses her purity and opportunity to marry a respectable man, Martine is obsessed that Sophie should have what the Tonton Macoutes stole from her—chastity and marriage to a successful man. As Carolle Charles notes in her essay "Gender and Politics in Contemporary Haiti: The Duvalierist State, Transnationalism, and the Emergence of a New Feminism (1980-1990)," for "most women cross culturally, in Haiti, marriage often determines or solidifies a woman's class position and not exceptionally, the majority of elite Haitian women gain or maintain their class position through marriage" (142). In order to ensure Sophie's purity and respectability for marriage, Martine performs "tests" to check for an unbroken hymen. She explains to Sophie that "a mother is supposed to do that to her daughter until the daughter is married. It is her responsibility to keep her pure" (Danticat 61). For Sophie, the tests are an attempt to control her sexuality as well as a violation of her body: "I closed my eyes upon the images of my mother slipping her hand under the sheets and poking her pinky at a void, hoping that it would go no further than the length of her fingernail" (155). Martine inflicts sexual testing upon Sophie, even though she knows women hate it because they "scream like a pig in a slaughterhouse" (60). Hence, Martine—herself a survivor of sexual abuse—contributes to the continuous cycle of sexual violence against Haitian women as acknowledged by Sophie's pain during the tests.

To cope with the testing, Sophie learns to "double" by disconnecting her mind with her body and thinking of "pleasant things" (155). Her dissociative episodes give her "a means of mental escape at the moment when no other escape is possible" (Herman 239) and a strategy of denying her sexual victimization at the hands of her mother. In an attempt to regain control over her body and end the weekly tests, Sophie decides to take a pestle and force it into her vagina to break her hymen. She succeeds in "failing" the next chastity test, but is forced by Martine to leave the household. Sophie seeks solace in a hasty marriage to her boyfriend; however, her memories of sexual abuse plague her relationship and generate negative associations of her body image and sexual contact. Like Martine, she is herself a victim of a history/tradition of sexual violations yet she is silenced by her mother into denying that history and not acknowledging her abusers.

For Sophie and Martine to end their nightmares of sexual abuse they return to Haiti to face a "place where nightmares are passed on through generation like heirlooms" (Danticat 234). Sophie starts her healing by confronting her mother about the tests and later accepting her explanation: "'I did it,' she [Martine] said, 'because my mother had done it to me. I have no greater excuse. I realize standing here that the two greatest pains of my life are very much related. The one good thing about being raped was that it made the testing stop. The testing and the rape. I live both every day'" (170). Sophie also returns to the cane field where Martine was raped. Her grandmother and aunt watch her catharsis in the field and acknowledge Sophie's liberation from sexual violence. They both call out, "'Ou libéré'—Are you free?" (Danticat 234). Before Sophie can answer their question, her grandmother puts her fingers over Sophie's lips and tells her, "'Now, you will know how to answer,'" meaning that she can release her sexual trauma and disturbing memories (234).

Danticat adds to the reconstruction of Haiti's history of violence by once again depicting the Tonton Macoutes as menacing oppressors in *The Dew Breaker*. The text centers upon the horrific acts of one particular Macoute called a "dew breaker," a torturer who arrives early in the morning, "breaks" the dew on the grass, and performs so well that his "victims were never able to speak of [him] again" (77). When the Dew Breaker named Mr. Bienaime admits his former profession of killing people to his daughter Ka, the story shifts from his current life in Brooklyn as a barber to the past visions of Haiti in 1967 and focuses on the horrifying acts of the Macoutes and the Duvalier legacy.

In the chapter titled "The Funeral Singer," the narrator and her two friends are victims of the Tonton Macoutes' brutal acts. The speaker recollects how her friend Mariselle fled Haiti because she feared for her safety: "Her husband, a painter, had painted an unflattering portrait of the president, which was displayed in a gallery show. He was shot leaving the show" (Danticat 172). The speaker's other friend, Rézia, was also forced to migrate from Haiti. While living with an aunt who owned a brothel, a "uniformed man" rapes her. Rézia later learns that her aunt was threatened with prison if "she didn't let him have [her] that night" (173). Like her friends, the narrator must depart from Haiti after she refuses to sing at the national palace. Her mother cautions her that her behavior will result in revenge by the Macoutes, and in addition, the narrator recognizes the power the Macoutes have to make people disappear: "But I'd also left because long ago my father had disappeared. He'd had a fish stall at the market. One day, one macoute came to take it over and another one took my father away" (172).

Moving from the reconstruction of memory to action, Danticat illustrates the Haitian citizens' attempt to regain control over the government in the chapter of "Monkey Tails." After enduring the years of hardship under the Duvalier regime, the characters in this section of the text welcome the exile of President "Baby Doc" Duvalier. As part of their celebration, they battle the Macoutes who had protected the Duvaliers and executed their atrocious commands. During one such incident, they "tie one of these militiamen to a lamppost, pour gasoline down his throat, and set him on fire" (140). At another confrontation, the citizens ravage the crypt of Papa Doc and parade around with his bones. While the citizens relish in their newfound freedom, the joy is short-lived because Haiti perishes around them: "the looting of homes and businesses of former government allies, the lynching, burning, and stoning of the macoutes, the thousands of bodies that were suddenly being discovered in secret rooms at the city morgues and in mass graves on the outskirts of the capital" (161-162).

Once "Baby Doc" Duvalier was ousted from power, many Tonton Macoutes fled Haiti because of the great risk of facing death by other Haitians. After migration, however, the former Macoutes still feared that revelation of their true identity would lead to their deaths. Likewise, Mr. Bienaime worries that his violent past will be exposed and cause his demise. In order to escape detection, he loses eighty pounds, changes his name and his birth place when he meets people, and refuses to pose for pictures. Mr. Bienaime also has no close friends or visitors, never discusses Haitian relatives, and never teaches Ka about Haiti (21). He successfully manages to avoid exposure, until a man named Dany recognizes him. Danticat tells Dany's story in "Night Talkers" and describes how Mr. Bienaime had killed Dany's parents and threatened his life:

> "He was six years old [. . .] and had been at home with his parents and his aunt, [. . .] when they heard a loud crash outside. His father went out first, followed by his mother. Dany was about to go after them when he heard the shots. [. . .] Behind him the front door was covered in flames.

"Shut up now or I'll shoot you too!" someone was shouting from the street.
It was a large man with a face like a soccer ball and a widow's peak dipping into
the middle of his forehead. The man was waving a gun at him [. . .]. (105)

Now years later, Dany plans to fulfill the promise that he has made to his
parents to kill their killer, Mr. Bienaime. He contemplates the various methods
of murdering him, but fears that he might have the wrong person. This doubt
prevents him from taking the life of Mr. Bienaime because he recognizes that
one person's actions affect a chain of people.

The Dew Breaker ends with Mr. Bienaime's last assassination of a Baptist
preacher who openly condemns Duvalier's policies. The preacher suffers
endless physical abuse by the Macoutes: they kick him with their boots, rub
cigarette butts in his hair, give him electric shocks, drag him to peel away his
skin, and finally shoot him multiple times. Nevertheless, before the preacher
dies, he stabs Mr. Bienaime on the cheek and intentionally leaves a visible
scar—a reminder of his deplorable actions. Danticat also reveals how the Dew
Breaker began his career as a Tonton Macoute because of the free goods and
domination over others. With a lust for more power, Mr. Bienaime becomes
legendary for discovering the "most physically and psychologically taxing trials
for the prisoners" (197):

> He liked to paddle them with braided cowhide, stand on their cracking backs and
> jump up and down like a drunk on a trampoline, pound a rock on the protruding
> bone behind their earlobes until they couldn't hear the orders he was shouting at
> them, tie blocks of concrete to the end of the sisal ropes and balance them on
> their testicles if they were men or their breasts if they were women. (198).

He justifies such use of violence to free Haitians from "brainwashing" and to
"return [them] to their ancestral beliefs" (188). However, his "blunt, ropelike
scar" which goes from the "right cheek down to the corner of [the] mouth" (5)
causes the Dew Breaker "to look like a monster" (239). Hence, his hideous
physical appearance mirrors his contemptible violations.

Danticat's Breath, Eyes, and Memory and The Dew Breaker criticize the
turbulent period in Haiti's history. This period is marked by the violent legacy
of the Duvalier regime and the Tonton Macoutes who lead a campaign of terror,
especially with the use of sexual violence against Haitian women and torture of
political dissenters. Out of fear, many Haitians did not voice their suffering
publicly and added to the unnamed and unpunished crimes of the Tonton
Macoutes. Through the stories in Danticat's texts, the violent past of Haiti
comes to the public's awareness and illustrates the suffering of Haitians as the
suffering of an entire community, a community that is attempting to heal
through telling its own story.

Works Cited

Charles, Carolle. "Gender and Politics in Contemporary Haiti: The Duvalierist State, Transnationalism, and the Emergence of a New Feminism (1980-1990)." *Feminist Studies* 21.1 (1995): 135-64.

Danticat, Edwidge. *Breath, Eyes, Memory.* New York: Vintage, 1994.

—. *The Dew Breaker.* New York: Vintage, 2004.

Fuller, Anne. "Challenging Violence: Haitian Women Unite Women's Rights and Human Rights." *Association of Concerned Africa Scholars* 55-56 (1999): 39-48.

Francis, Donette A. "'Silences Too Horrific to Disturb': Writing Sexual Histories in Edwidge Danticat's *Breath, Eyes, Memory.*" *Research in African Literatures* 35.2 (2004): 75-90.

Herman, Judith Lewis. *Trauma and Recovery.* New York: Basic Books, 1992.

Hillman, Richard S., and Thomas J. D'Agostino, eds. *Understanding the Contemporary Caribbean.* Boulder: Lynne Rienner Publishers, 2003.

Worthington, Kim L. *Self as Narrative: Subjectivity and Community in Contemporary Fiction.* Oxford: Clarendon Press, 1996.

TALES OF SOUND AND FURY: WOMEN IN MERLINDA BOBIS'S *WHITE TURTLE*

LIBE GARCÍA ZARRANZ

> ... To love in a language prised between one's wishbone. To sing of a landscape where village girls once burst the moon with giggles. To dance through the fattest eye of a ricegrain...
>
> Merlinda Bobis, *Summer was a Fast Train without Terminals*

From the 1970s onwards, the redefinition of women's position in literature and society has been one of the main concerns for writers and critics within the field of postcolonial studies. The contributions made by authors of the stature of Toni Morrison or Gayatri Chakravorty Spivak refer to different geopolitical spaces such as India or the United States and yet, their conclusions share some illuminating points that might help us better understand the situations lived by women in diverse postcolonial communities.[1]

Taking these ideas as a starting point, this essay attempts to analyze the complex significance of some of the female characters portrayed in Merlinda Bobis's short-story collection *White Turtle* (1999). As a Filipino-Australian writer, Bobis stands as a "translator," to quote her own words, and thus benefits from a privileged perspective of Eastern and Western culture. Most of her stories are set in Iraya, a northern village in the Philippines from which female voices, marginalized under colonial oppression and patriarchy, are now given a chance to be heard. Nevertheless, Australia is also selected as the perfect scenario to explore other topics, such as the tensions emerging from writing on the margins.

Having said this, I would like to focus my study on the two key issues of sexuality and identity, which in turn address other aspects such as motherhood,

---

[1] See Toni Morrison's *Playing in the Dark* (1992) and Gayatri Chakravorty Spivak's *A Critique of Postcolonial Reason: Toward a History of the Vanishing Present* (1999).

power structures, the role of silence, and the construction of a "displaced" self. A starting point for this analysis is the family structures displayed in Bobis's collection. The secrecy surrounding father figures and the absence of mothers make the figure of the female orphan a recurrent theme in many of the stories. On the one hand, we might look for a sociological explanation, if we take into account these alarming figures: approximately 4,100 to 4,900 women and girls die each year in the Philippines due to pregnancy-related complications.[2] On the other hand, if we turn our attention to literary traditions, we discover that orphan figures have pervaded worldwide fiction, from traditional fairy tales to Dickens's unforgettable creations in Victorian England. Furthermore, novels such as *Uncle Tom's Cabin* (1851-52) by Harriet Beecher Stowe or Toni Morrison's *Beloved* (1987) also explore images of orphanhood to portray the disempowerment and disavowal of the African American community. What is it that makes orphans such fascinating figures? According to Melanie Kimball, "Orphans embody loneliness—they do not belong. Orphans symbolize the feeling of abandonment that all humans experience at times. BUT orphans in literature also give us hope" (1). In Bobis's stories, female orphans are usually portrayed as victims of their own absent mothers in one way or another. In "The Sadness Collector," we find six-year-old Rica, who was abandoned by her mother when she was three as she had to cross the ocean to get a living as domestic helper. However, secrecy pervades the story, so the reader is left without actually knowing what has happened to the mother. Similarly, in "The Curse," we find Eya, a bald orphan girl who lives with Dulce, her surrogate mother. Her hairlessness is explained by the Catholic community as "God's punishment of the mother, which has been inherited by her bastard daughter" (Bobis 62). Later on in the story, we find out that Eya's mother was a teenager who died in childbirth and then was implicitly condemned as a sinner and compared to the figure of Mary Magdalene. The father's identity, however, is not revealed, although there are several hints in the narrative which point to Pay Inyo, ironically described as "the Mister Hol-arawnd of Iraya—their "all-around" man, their Jack-of-all-trades" (69). This man "feels overwhelmed under [Dulce's] knowing gaze" (62) and he has "stopped meeting [Dulce's] eyes lest she betray the unspoken" (75). These comments make the reader suspect this male figure of possibly being Eya's father. Once again, abused young women are forever marked with an eternal scar and judged under patriarchy, whereas men's acts are left unquestioned in a society structured around a double morality.

On the other hand, some of these orphan girls make the community feel

---

[2] Data taken from the Maternal and Neonatal Program Effort Index in http://www.policyproject.com

uneasy by their disturbing presence, as they are "clearly marked as being different from the rest of society. They are the eternal Other" (Kimball 1). In "Pina and the Flying Cross," the community describes 6-year-old Pina as "a little devil" and argues: "She is a strange one [...] always playing alone or following her grandmother around. That's what happens when a child doesn't even know who her father is" (Bobis 100). Notice that the child also seems to be carrying the burden of her mother's "sinful" sexuality, as she is constructed as "loose as a skirt missing its elastic" (100). Likewise, in "The Kissing," we hear about the story of Clarita's mother, often referred to by the villagers as "the wild Asuncion" or as a "slut," since she abandoned her child and her husband for a white American man. Here again we find derogatory references to women, always defined and indicted in terms of their sexuality.

In Bobis's stories, we also find young girls who explicitly justify their mother's absence as a defence mechanism in order to survive. Connie, the young narrator in "Flores de Mayo," explains her identity in the following terms:

> Grandmother says I was not rightfully named. That I am not her *consuelo*—not her joy or consolation, but her despair. Like my mother. But I'm not a bad girl, believe me. And I don't think Mother is all that bad either. She's just too busy to visit (161).

Connie's own defense is intimately linked to the unconditional recognition and justification of her mother's goodness. Later on, we find out that her mother is coming home pregnant, which will complicate the mother-daughter relationship even further.

Bobis's orphan children, however, seem to have acquired a powerful identity out of their need to survive. Most of them have developed an extraordinary imagination which characterizes their unique personality. In "Pina and the Flying Cross," set in Iraya in 1945, we find the little girl Pina challenging the Catholic community by refusing to believe that the object they have seen in the sky is a flying cross. Instead, she believes it is a dragonfly with huge burning eyes, which shocks the women believers. Likewise, Connie, in "Flores de Mayo," refuses to collect white flowers for the Virgin since she thinks white is a boring colour: "I wonder if she ever gets bored at our lack of imagination as we litter her aisle with petals and petals of only white" (160). It should be stressed that whiteness has different connotations in the stories. On the one hand, it symbolizes women's virginity for the Catholic community. Then, in stories such as "White Turtle," this color is associated with the act of storytelling and the oral tradition.[3] On the other hand, the white color stands for

---

[3] See Maria Dolores Herrero Granado's article "Merlinda Bobis's Use of Magic Realism

the footprint of the colonizer, embodied by Spanish and American imperial power in stories such as "Pina and the Flying Cross," where an American pilot is ironically described as "white as the angels [...] So white...all blood must have left him" (106-107). In conclusion, we could argue that the strong identity of these orphan girls functions as a mighty source of resistance to the rigid morality of the Catholic Church, understood as a remnant of Spanish colonization.

So far, we have identified several images of orphanhood pervading Bobis's narrative. In most of the stories, both mothers and fathers are absent. Who then represents authority? It is the figure of the grandmother that achieves relevance and power. To start with, grandmothers are portrayed as witnesses and victims of colonization. In "Fruit Stall," we hear a granddaughter talking about the origins of her family:

> I dyed my hair brown. It goes well with this pale skin from my Spanish grandfather whom I never saw. He owned the hacienda where my grandmother served as housemaid. They sent her away when she grew a melon under her skirt (4).

These comments illustrate unbalanced power relations and women's lower position in a society ruled by patriarchy and colonization. Besides, the woman, as happened with most pregnant single women in the Philippines up to the late 1990s, is punished, becoming a social outcast.

In Bobis's stories, grandmothers are also depicted as symbol of tradition in Philippine culture. Inday's grandmother in "Border Lover" becomes one of Bobis's most hilarious creations. She strongly defends her native language against the "strange tongue" her granddaughter speaks in Australia. She enjoys the "comfort of tropical domesticity" and above all, she loves her cooking: "LEAVE MY STOVE ALONE" (125) she exclaims after her granddaughter has tried to sell her a discourse on "silly piminism," as she calls it.

Alternatively, grandmothers are portrayed in Bobis's tales as supporters of the status quo through their silence and their myths on women's sexuality. In "The Curse," Eya's grandmother decides, when her teenage daughter dies at childbirth, that it is "best to keep the poor dear out of it, best to keep silent, then the rest of Iraya will hush its malicious murmurings" (73). Similarly, in "Flores de Mayo," Connie's grandma teaches her a distorted lesson on female sexuality and pregnancy:

> Grandmother says the well spirits always keep watch from below, so one must

---

as Reflected in 'White Turtle'" for a detailed interpretation of the story. *Revista Alicantina de Estudios Ingleses* 16 (2003): 1-46.

never bathed completely naked. They can blow air into your vagina and you
might bloat [...] I wonder whether Mother ever bathed naked near a well. The
last time she visited, her tummy looked strange (165).

The result of mixing religious myths and legends with pregnancy is terribly
dangerous, as it contributes to reinforcing taboos and ignorance around
women's sexuality. Besides, this lack of information prevents women from
being aware of their own bodies and of the possibilities contraceptive measures
bring about.

Finally, grandmothers are represented as the matriarchs of the community.
Lola Conching illustrates this idea in the story of "Pina and the Flying Cross":
"The women huddled close, *like hurt orphans.* Lola Conching is walking away,
just like that?" (100, my emphasis). Lola is rendered a referent for the female
community in Iraya, becoming a symbolic Mother figure.[4]

As I have endeavored to demonstrate, the recurrence of grandmother figures
in *White Turtle* is significant as they occupy a crucial role in Philippine society.
It is worth mentioning that in an interview, Bobis referred to her grandmother as
the person who had greatly influenced her as a writer: "Mama Ola, my maternal
grandmother. The grandmothers, wise women and shamans in my stories are
drawn from her."[5]

Having explored family structures in Bobis's stories, I would like to move
on to analyze the representation of some of the female characters in relation to
the concept of the *fetish*. Laura Mulvey, applying Freud's ideas[6] to the
cinematic gaze and giving them a gender focus, introduces *fetishistic
scopophilia* or a way of looking which "builds up the physical beauty of the
object, transforming it into something satisfying in itself" (Visual 21). The
female image is thus idealized, becoming an object of contemplation. The role
of Señorita Clarita, one of the female characters in the "The Kissing," could
function as an interesting starting point to illustrate the relation established
between the *fetish* and the construction of femininity. In this story, Clarita is
only an image decorating Don Miguel Balaguer's gloomy *comidor*: "[She]
would never be able to walk out of her father's canvas sitting at the head of the
table" (Bobis 87). Metaphorically trapped within patriarchy, Clarita is never
given a voice in the narrative. Instead, the reader listens to her story through
Manolito, a 16-year-old cook who is fascinated by the young girl in the portrait.
Therefore, the image of the woman becomes the perfect fetishistic object.

---

[4] The figure of an old woman as symbol for the Mother Nation has pervaded the pages of
postcolonial literature in countries such as Ireland or India, in writers like William Trevor
and Salman Rushdie.
[5] "An interview with Merlinda Bobis" in http://www.auntlute.com/bobisinterview.html.
[6] See Freud's essay "Instincts and their Vicissitudes" (1915).

"Jar" is another of Bobis's tales which could also be examined in terms of the fetish. The Oxford Dictionary defines fetish as "an inanimate object worshipped for its supposed magical powers" or "a form of sexual desire in which gratification is focused abnormally on an object, part of the body, or activity."[7] The female character in this story makes recurrent references to the jar exhibited in the antique shop where she works, revealing an implicit complicity with the object: "Tomorrow, I get sacked. The jar and I understand what this means, and what then needs to be done" (Bobis 152). These opening lines establish the intimate connection constructed between the woman and the object she has idealized. Throughout the story, she polishes the jar, rubs it and she even talks to it. In the story, the jar is red and it is at display, locked in a cupboard for exhibition. There is a process of identification between the commodity and the woman, as both are touched and contemplated. Furthermore, a jar is an object which can be filled up, a container that parallels patriarchal constructions of the female body. In the eyes of her boss, she has become a fetish herself. Yet, the woman is pregnant and in consequence, her representation is modified and is transformed into a source of *abjection*. In *Powers of Horror*, Julia Kristeva defines "abjection" as that which does not "respect borders, positions, rules," that which "disturbs identity, system, order" (4). She then expands the term and applies it to the construction of the maternal figure as abject from the moment the child wants to separate itself from her body at an early stage. In "Jar," the female body shifts from being a site of sexual pleasure to becoming a site of anxiety, as the protagonist anticipates. Once he knows she is pregnant, "[h]is hand will drop. Panic will leap out of his eyes to smother the part of my anatomy in question. 'You were not careful?' He will shred the room with gestures" (Bobis 153). Notice that he distances himself from her now "polluted" body which becomes an agent of fear. As Mulvey explains: "When the exterior carapace of feminine beauty collapses to reveal the uncanny, abject maternal body it is as though the fetish itself has failed" (*Fetishism* 14). However, the narrative has an unexpected turn when the reader finds out that the woman's belly is growing a black mouth with prominent teeth in its navel. These images echo the myth of the *vagina dentata* or toothed vagina, which has prevailed as a recurrent motif in folklore, literature, psychoanalysis, cinema and painting. The image of the *vagina dentata* has been interpreted on a double basis: woman as castrator/ woman as castrated. For my analysis of Bobis's story I will focus on the castrating woman as a powerful punishing agent which transgresses patriarchal modes of representation, since the intention of the female protagonist in "Jar" is to devour the male body:

---

[7] Oxford Dictionary Online in http://www.askoxford.com/concise_oed/fetish?view=uk

His little finger will get stuck [...] then the hand, the arm, the shoulder, the screaming head, the struggling upper torso, then the pelvis that will have lost what little bulge it had [...] all will be swallowed up. He will disappear (Bobis 156).

The protagonist reverses the situation she had previously experienced with the old man, which consisted in exchanging her body and sexuality for a job.[8] She had been figuratively swallowed by him and now, she takes revenge. Note that she even questions her masculinity through the reference to the size of his sexual organ. In her analysis of the monstrous-feminine in film, Barbara Creed explains that woman as castrator takes at least three forms: "Woman as the deadly *femme castrati*, the castrating mother and the *vagina dentata*" (7). Bobis cleverly combines the three figures to shape a powerful female character that transgresses the reader's expectations, creating a disturbing imagery.

Creed's insights are also useful to examine the female character in "Fish-Hair Woman," who undergoes a series of physical transformations which turn her from an exotic commodity into an agent of fear and monstrosity: "my twelve metres of very thick black hair with its streaks of red [...] I had come to be such a *freak of nature*" (11-12, my emphasis). Her ambivalence could be associated, not only to the western myth of the female figure of Medusa, but also, according to Carolyn Brewer, to "the powerful female shaman *baylan* or *catalonan* of the pre-Hispanic Tagalog and Visayan speaking areas of the Philippines" (Brewer 2).

Historically, patriarchal ideology has sustained the symbolic image of woman as an enigma, often surrounded by a halo of mystery and secrecy, while simultaneously depriving her of the possibility of self-definition: "Imaginatively [woman] is of the highest importance; practically she is completely insignificant. She pervades poetry from cover to cover; she is all but absent from history" (Woolf 45). In the story "Fish Hair Woman," the female narrator makes an explicit comment on her own experience of being constructed by a man's imagination as a goddess: "I suspected that the sergeant had slyly desired me, maybe even worshipped me" (19). It has been argued that the ambivalence in the portrayal of women as either virgins or whores is a patriarchal construction designed to maintain the status quo. Women must be either contemplated as objects of desire of the male gaze or repudiated as agents of fear and therefore, transgression: "He only stared at my brown body in the wet *tapis*, then at my face, always at my face" (19). It is worth pinpointing the distinction between "looking" and "being-looked-at," following Laura Mulvey's ideas in her much-quoted essay "Visual Pleasure": "In a world ordered by sexual imbalance,

---

[8] There is a phrase in the Philippines that sums up the sexual violence experienced by women in the workplace which is the "Lie Down or Lay Off Policy."

pleasure in looking has been split between active/male and passive/female" (19). The woman in the story is placed at the very centre of attention, thus becoming an exotic object of desire for the male gaze. Besides, she is captured in fragments, intensifying her passive construction and fetishism.

The woman in Bobis's story is known and addressed by different names: she, woman, fisherwoman, Hair of Estrella and Fish-Hair Woman. The multiple quality of identity in the story alludes to a metaphorical loss and disorientation of the subject and the self. There are hints that point out that her identity is in a process of development. Through the words of the narrator, Bobis, self-consciously, might be addressing the idea of speaking from the margins: "A *strange voice*, sorrow *creeping at the edges*. I realised it was mine" (14, my emphasis). It seems there is a process of adjustment and recognition of one's identity.

Nevertheless, the female character in "Fish-Hair Woman" is the narrator of the story and therefore, she is in control, not only of the progression of the narrative, but also of the point of view. It is through her voice that the reader recognizes her and her world: "No, *I* will not allow you to invent me, too, you who read this, so *I* will tell you everything" (13, my emphasis). She exclaims "no," refusing to accept constructions, as she is the owner of her own identity and life. Her "I" is empowered through storytelling and writing: "Print, in obliterating the need for memory, inevitably contains and fixes the past [...] but it also creates marginal spaces in which the silenced voices of totalizing systems can speak" (Slemon 418). In this sense, "Jar" also portrays a female character with an empowered identity. The protagonist herself is determined to tell the reader of her plans and thus, to be heard. She anticipates for the reader privileged information that only she possesses, since the narrative is fully told from her point of view.

As previously demonstrated, female voices are a key element in Bobis's stories. Nevertheless, *White Turtle* should also be analyzed in terms of its silences. It is in stories such as "The Sadness Collector" that the unspoken becomes central: "She breathes easier [...] eyes still wary and a mouth forming the old, silent question–are you really there?" (129-130). Through several references to silence, Bobis creates a powerful effect on the reader, who becomes aware of the importance of reading between the lines: "she's actually checking the plates now [...] peeking into cups of sadness, both overt and unspoken" (130). Furthermore, the technique of combining external narration with free indirect style, allows the girl in the story to speak; she is given a voice. Therefore, the reader must look beyond surfaces and interpret the complex layers of authority and power in narrative terms.

Many women characters in the collection *White Turtle* have been victims of male exploitation and abuse and, as a result, their bodies and voices have been silenced. The reason for this situation is understandable if we take into account that traditional gender roles in Filipino society are "strongly influenced by centuries of Islamic culture, Chinese mores, and 425 years of deep-rooted Spanish Catholic traditions."[9] In the story called "Shoes," we are told about Trining:

> After the flood, Nito offered his sister, Nestor's wife, as a housemaid for the master in exchange for her family's temporary shelter on his farm. And "temporary" became forever. (Bobis 117-118)

The woman is portrayed as "sister," "wife" and "mother" but the reader does not have the opportunity to hear her voice as Trining. As Shoshana Felman explained, "To 'speak in the name of,' to 'speak *for*,' could thus mean, once again, to appropriate and to silence" (Eagleton 36). It is Nestor, her husband, who goes with their little daughter to the master's house to claim Trining, a woman who has been offered to Mr. Jose, a 74-year-old man, as a commodity. Likewise, the narrator in "Fruit Stall" explains how foreign men are attracted to the Philippines to find cheap women to have sex with: "Sample the merchandise. This is how the men, who go to my country to find themselves a nice, little brown girl, put it" (Bobis 5). Filipino women are thus placed under a multiple trap based on gender discrimination, racism and class. In the story of "Storm," the reader witnesses how Viring, again a maid, is raped by her "master," a white man:

> [M]y bruised breasts, the blood between my thighs, on his limp thing and all over my blanket…and more coconuts fronds than I could ever imagine, peering down through that hole on the roof […] Even when I shut my eyes the whole time he grunted like a pig on top of me, I saw his face clearly, even his eyes (35).

The young woman describes the violent scene using a wide variety of images of her own body. Then, she uses metaphors to associate the act of sexual abuse with coconuts, a typical fruit in the Philippines. Viring, dragged away from her childhood, family and habitat, has experienced an allegorical fall into maturity. Like the coconuts she imagines, Viring has not undergone a natural process of development and growth. Instead, a violent storm has shaken her body and her heart. Washed away from her origins, Viring cannot possibly go back again. Notice that the image of the long trunk of a coconut tree produces a distancing effect, due to its proportions, which could be associated to the idea of dispossession. Furthermore, it should be noted that the coconut tree is known as

---

[9] *The International Encyclopedia of Sexuality* in http://www2.huberlin.de/sexology/IES/philippines.html#1

"the tree of life" so, while the coconuts hang in the tree, they could symbolize the Mother Nation in a stage of pre-colonization. Yet, once the first coconut has fallen, the colonized peoples are disempowered and as a result, they bleed and suffer: "My heart had sucked it all in through its red mouth, a tiny hole the width of a coconut frond" (36). The image of the "red mouth" could stand for the woman's vagina, reinforcing the idea of rape. It is worth mentioning that the Philippines had been imagined for more than three centuries of Spanish rule as "*terre nourrice*" (Anderson 65). The French term *nourrice*, meaning "one who nourishes," reinforces the idea of the Philippines as nurturing Mother Nation.

Finally, yet another tale in *White Turtle* which explores gender roles in an unsettling tone: in "Yellow," we find a woman left at home while her husband goes on one of his frequent long trips. The woman is confined within the household, while the man occupies the public realm of business and economy. Before parting, her husband leaves her a yellow chick "to amuse" her (109). Far from entertaining her, his present becomes a disturbing element and a source of anxiety for the woman: "[The chicken's] breathing filled the room. She couldn't stand the sound of yellow breathing within an enclosed space, so she left the room, the house" (109). Yellow is a color that has been recurrently used in multiple stories to symbolize different forms of woman's oppression. In 1892, the American Charlotte Perkins Gilman published "The Yellow Wall-paper," based on her own experience of confinement. The story presents a white middle class woman driven to insanity by a domineering husband. Gradually, the female protagonist begins to project her own anxieties onto the yellow wall paper of the room where she remains in physical and intellectual prostration. The color then is identified with the oppression suffered by women under patriarchy.

Likewise, the color yellow also appears, with various connotations, in Jamaica Kincaid's *Lucy* (1990). The female protagonist in the novel is a young black woman from the Caribbean who moves to the USA to work as an au pair for a white family. According to Moira Ferguson, "[For Lucy,] the colour yellow is [linked] with painful memories of her mother that interact with pernicious colonial signs. Yellow is the jaundiced marker of white cultural identity" (François 90). Although differently, yellow becomes in the three stories a symbol of female subjugation.

To conclude, I would like to stress that Merlinda Bobis is not alone in her attempt to denounce women's situation in the Philippines through literature. The Filipino writer Gina Abuyan-Llane has also explored the tensions between men and the female body in her shattering short story "The Fruit Women":

My husband tells me of a place where men can pick off women from the trees, like fruits ripened in season, and have them, suckle at them, sip and bite at them, as they will. The women do not complain [...] as they were born–blossomed–to be this way.[10]

The beginning of Gina's tale certainly illustrates some of the constructed notions embodied and figured in male recurrent fantasies of the female body; ideas upon which Bobis insists throughout the stories in her collection. By focusing on two essential aspects such as identity and sexuality, the women in the tales abandon their marginal spaces to be relocated at the fore of the narrative. Women, nonetheless, not only need to conquer their own body and space but also to command storytelling; to be the owners of voice and tale in order to master narratives and accordingly write their own lives and futures to avoid what Gilbert and Gubar interpreted as the controlling mechanism of literary paternity (1979). Bobis succeeds in giving voice to a myriad variety of complex and fascinating female characters ranging from little orphans and wise grandmothers to abused and exploited women by presenting their particular stories as "activators of change" (Warner 210). Therefore, if we readers spread out our senses carefully, we will be able to see, smell and hear the sound of women's voices in Bobis's tales of love and fury.

Works Cited

Anderson, Benedict. *The Spectre of Comparisons: Nationalism, Southeast Asia, and the World*. London and New York: Verso, 1998.

Bobis, Merlinda. *White Turtle*. North Australia: Spinifex Press, 1999.

Brewer, Carolyn, "Merlinda Bobis, *White Turtle*". *Intersections: Gender, History and Culture in the Asian Context*, issue 4, September 2000, <http://wwwsshe.murdoch.edu.au/intersections/issue4/turtle.html.>

Creed, Barbara. *The Monstrous-Feminine*. London and New York: Routledge, 1993.

Eagleton, Mary. *Feminist Literary Theory: A Reader*. Oxford and New York: Basil Blackwell, 1986.

François, Irline. "The Daffodil Gap: Jamaica Kincaid's *Lucy*" *Journal of the Association of Caribbean Women Writers and Scholars* 4 (2001): 84-100.

Gilbert, Sandra. M and Susan Gubar. *The Madwoman in the Attic: The Woman Writer and the Nineteenth-Century Literary Imagination*. New Haven and London: Yale UP, 1979.

Herrero Granado, Maria Dolores. "Merlinda Bobis's Use of Magic Realism as

---

[10] Quotation from Modern Wife: http://www.modernwife.com/fruit-women.html

Reflected in 'White Turtle.'" *Revista Alicantina de Estudios Ingleses* 16, November 2003. 1-46.

Kimball, Melanie. A. "From Folktales to Fiction: Orphan Characters in Children's Literature." *Library Trends*. 47.3 (1999): 558-578.

Kristeva, Julia. *Powers of Horror: An Essay on Abjection*. Trans. Leon S. Roudiez. New York: Columbia UP, 1982

Morrison, Tony. *Playing in the Dark*. London: Picador, 1992.

Mulvey, Laura. *Fetishism and Curiosity*. London: British Film Institute Publishing, 1996.

—. *Visual and Other Pleasures*. Bloomington and Indianapolis: Indiana University Press, 1989.

Slemon, Stephen. "Magic Realism as Postcolonial Discourse." *Magical Realism: Theory, History, Community*. Eds. Lois Parkinson Zamora and Wendy B. Faris. Durham and London: Duke University Press, 1995. 407-26.

Spivak, Gayatri Chakravorty. *A Critique of Postcolonial Reason: Toward a History of the Vanishing Present*. USA: Harvard U. P, 1999.

Warner, Marina. *Fantastic Metamorphoses, Other Worlds*. New York: OUP, 2002.

Woolf, Virginia. *A Room of One's Own*. London: Penguin Books, 1945.

"An Interview with Merlinda Bobis." <http://www.auntlute.com/bobisinterview.html>.

CONTRIBUTORS

Nandita Batra was born in Bombay (now Mumbai) and received a B.A. and M.A. from the University of Delhi and a Ph.D. from the University of Rochester. Her main areas of interest lie in nineteenth-century British literature, particularly in Anthrozoological Studies. She is Professor of English at the University of Puerto Rico-Mayagüez, where she is also editor of *Revista Atenea*, the University's bilingual journal of humanities and social sciences. Recent publications include *Transgression and Taboo* (CEA-CC 2005) and *This Watery World: Humans and the Sea* (Cambridge Scholars Publishing 2008).

Matthew O. Cleveland teaches with the Program of Writing & Rhetoric at the University of Colorado, Boulder. Dr. Cleveland's broad teaching repertoire includes having conducted courses in 19th and 20th Century American and British literature, film and literature, gender and race issues in literature, critical theory, and rhetoric. With a focus upon engaging ethical issues in 20th Century literature and culture, Dr. Cleveland has published work in the fields of psychoanalysis, cultural studies, film studies, popular culture, and postcolonialism.

Darrell Fike is an associate professor of English at Valdosta State University in Georgia. His academic and creative writing have appeared in various anthologies and journals including *Elements of Alternate Style, The Subject is Reading, The Dissertation and the Discipline, College Composition and Communication, Thirteen Ways of Looking for a Poem, College English, The New Delta Review, The Ledge, Birmingham Poetry Review*, and others. His research interests include exploring the boundaries and intersections of creative and critical writing.

Libe García Zarranz is a PhD Fellow at the University of Alberta (Canada). She is currently engaged in doctoral research on contemporary Canadian women writers. García has published on the representation of women in contemporary authors William Trevor and Merlinda Bobis. She serves on the editorial board for the University of Puerto Rico's *Revista Atenea* and is guest co-editor of the second issue of *The Raymond Carver Review* on "Carver and Feminism."

Jocelyn A. Géliga Vargas (Ph.D. Communications) is Assistant Professor in the Department of English at the University of Puerto Rico-Mayagüez. She has also taught in universities in Argentina and the US. Her areas of interest are feminist cultural studies; media and film studies; identity and representation; ethnography and oral history. Her publications include journal articles and book chapters on film studies, diasporic Puerto Rican identity and feminist ethnographic research. She is currently working on an oral history project on Afro-Puerto Rican identity supported by the Latin American Studies Association and the Faculty of Arts and Sciences at UPRM.

Nick Haydock is Professor of English at the University of Puerto Rico, Mayagüez where he has taught for the past fourteen years. He is the author of *Movie Medievalism: The Imaginary Middle Ages* (2008), co-guest editor (with Richard Burt) of a special edition of *Exemplaria* 19.2 on "Movie Medievalism" (2007), and co-editor (with E. L. Risden) of the forthcoming book *Hollywood in the Holy Land*. He has also has written a number of articles on late medieval literature. Current projects include a book on *The Place of Robert Henryson's Testament of Cresseid*, an edition of Gavin Douglas' *Eneados*, and a novel entitled *Quod Dunbar*.

Mary Leonard teaches film and literature at the University of Puerto Rico, Mayagüez Campus, and is coordinator of the Certificate in Film Studies. Her published articles include: "Art and Trauma: The Evolution of the Contemporary British Novel," "The Intellectual, the Literary, and Public Discourse," "What the Parrots Sing Of: The Literary Voyages of Alvaro Mutis and Fernando Vallejo," and "Towards a Diversification of the Media: New Community Radio and Television Projects in the Americas." She is the director of Optika: A Symposium on Visual Narration.

Vartan P. Messier was born in Geneva and has taught Literature, Film, French, and English in Europe and the U.S. as well as Central America and the Caribbean. He is now a Doctoral Candidate in Comparative Literature at the University of California at Riverside and his research focuses on the critical discourses on modernity, modernism, and postmodernism in literature and the visual arts. In addition to *Transgression and Taboo* (CEA-CC 2005), and *This Watery World* (Cambridge Scholars Publishing 2008), two essay collections co-edited with Nandita Batra, other recent publications have focused on cinematic transtextuality, narrativity and identity, as well as on consumerism and globalization.

Robert Miltner is Associate Professor of English at Kent State University Stark and teaches in the Northeast Ohio MFA in Creative Writing program. He edits *The Raymond Carver Review* and is co-editor of *New Paths to Raymond Carver: Critical Essays on His Life, Fiction, and Poetry* (University of South Carolina Press, 2008). A poet and short story writer, Miltner has written critical essays on James Joyce, Virginia Woolf, John Steinbeck, Campbell McGrath, Russell Edson, Jorie Graham, and Raymond Carver, as well as on prose poetry, literacy, artistic collaboration, and writing as cultural identity.

Christopher Powers (Ph.D. Johns Hopkins University, 2003) is Assistant Professor of Comparative Literature in the Humanities Department at the Mayagüez Campus of the University of Puerto Rico. His research and teaching interests include African American modernism, music and literature, and the nineteenth century prehistory of modernism. He has taught on jazz writing and written about the jazz essays of Ralph Ellison, the novels of Toni Morrison, and the musicology and philosophy of Theodor Adorno.

Dorsía Smith has a Ph.D. in Caribbean Literature and teaches English at the University of Puerto Rico, Río Piedras. She is currently co-editing *Caribbean without Borders: Literature, Language, and Culture* (Cambridge Scholars Press) and *Latina/Chicana Mothering* (Demeter Press). Her work has most recently appeared in *La Torre, Journal of the Association for Research on Mothering*, and the *African American National Biography*.

Tatiana A. Tagirova was born in Russia and received her Bachelor's in English from Novgorod State University in Russia. She went on to pursue a Master's in Education from Philadelphia Biblical University and a Doctoral degree in Caribbean Literature from the University of Puerto Rico at Rio Piedras. She approaches Claude McKay from the perspective of his reception in Russia. She has published articles in journals such as *Milenio, La Torre*, and *Tesolgram* and has presented her papers at different conferences both local and international. At the present moment she is an Assistant Professor at the University of Puerto Rico at Bayamón.

Don E. Walicek is a Ph.D. candidate in English linguistics at the University of Puerto Rico at Rio Piedras. The Managing Editor of the journal *Sargasso*, his primary academic interests are in Creole Studies, sociolinguistics, and the language-ideology interface. His publications include "The Founder Principle and Anguilla's Homestead Society" (John Benjamins in press), "Chinese Spanish in Nineteenth-Century Cuba: Documenting Sociohistorical Context"

(John Benjamins 2007), and "Farther South: Speaking American, The Language of Migration in Samaná" (University of Virginia Press 2007).

INDEX